HOW TO DISCOVER, OWN AND SHARE YOUR STORY WELL

Jennifer Spoelma

WORDS
MOVE
PEOPLE

To Mom and Dad
Thank you for raising me to know the Lord,
and for teaching me to follow where he leads.
I love you.

CONTENTS

Discover Your Story

Own Your Story

Share Your Story

Part One

DISCOVER YOUR STORY

CHAPTER ONE

What is Your Story?

How does the idea of explaining your faith to someone else make you feel? What about the idea of sharing your story? Does it make you cringe? Does it make your palms hot and sweaty? Or is talking about your faith an everyday occurrence for you? Are you always on the lookout for opportunities to talk about Jesus? Wherever you are on the spectrum, my guess is that your reaction to the idea of sharing the gospel is a strong one. Many of us experience conflict between the techniques we've been taught for sharing the gospel and our real-life interactions with people outside of the church. Maybe you've disagreed with a friend's method of evangelism. Maybe you've witnessed a speaker's method do more damage than good. Maybe you were taught to explain the gospel using an "ABC" method, a set of tracts or something similar that wasn't *wrong*, but felt insincere or cheap. These contradictory experiences can confuse Christians who are engaged with the outside world. We believe that sharing our faith is an integral part of our walk with God, yet our models for doing so may feel pushy or irrelevant.

However, by learning to communicate our vibrant relationship with Jesus in an authentic way, we can change this. The key is your personal story. Your story can demonstrate the life-changing nature and beauty of a relationship with Jesus. You can use your story to engage in genuine conversations with others, find common ground and explain the hope you have in Christ. Not only will knowing your story give you the confidence to explain your faith, but it will allow your story to resonate with others. Authenticity facilitates trust and breaks down the walls of skepticism and judgement. Your personal story of faith has much more potential to touch someone's heart than a perfectly-practiced gospel presentation or a convincing apologetics argument.

By definition, authenticity isn't something that can be faked. This is good news! You love the Lord. You believe that he is powerful, that he has forgiven you and set you free. Your faith *is* authentic. Jesus is your savior, and his presence in your life makes a huge difference. And because of that, you want others to know him too. You don't need a clever technique to share the gospel with others; you just need to feel confident in sharing your story. And that's what this book is all about. It's a guide for identifying how your faith intertwines with your unique life experiences. Once you feel confident in your story, you will be able to share your faith with authenticity.

Confidence in your story starts with valuing your life's journey. It requires taking all of the broken pieces—the messy ones along with the pretty ones—and reconciling them into a cohesive whole. It takes time, intention and hard work. Personally, journaling has proved to be the best way for me to process life's circumstances and glean meaning and purpose. Journaling has become my go-to for dealing with heartbreak, disappointments and hard questions.

DISCOVERING A STORYLINE

I wrote my first journal entry when I was 16 years old. After a failed relationship left me hurting, my older sister called me from college to see how I was doing. I cried, and told her how sad and confused I felt. She listened first, then asked me if I had been praying and talking to God about my feelings. I answered, "Kind of… I just don't know what to say." She suggested that I try journaling, as a way to write out my prayers and work through my feelings. I reluctantly agreed. "Okay, I'll try it."—and I did, even though I was skeptical it would help. Journaling was awkward at first. I didn't know what to write. I didn't know how to put my feelings into words, and I kept feeling like I needed to tear out pages every time I wrote something that sounded stupid or pathetic. But thankfully, I kept at it. I worked through hurt and frustrations on paper, and more importantly, in prayer with God. Instead of first running to friends to vent, I became more comfortable seeking God in prayer. For me, journaling was a catalyst for connecting my faith to my day-to-day life.

As time went on, I noticed a shift in my writing. Painful experiences still marked my journal entries, but they began to take on a different form. Instead of pain being the main focus, a sense of purpose and hope started shining through. Through journaling, I learned to reflect on my circumstances and tie them together to find meaning. I recognized that God really was at work in my life. He had been active and involved all along. He was, and is, transforming me into his image through the various circumstances he has led me through. And that process of challenge, followed by growth, is the very essence of story. Realizing that I had a story—unique and specially designed by God for me—transformed the way I live my life. It increased my faith, trust, discernment and understanding of God's call on my life. However, that's not the end game when it comes to understanding our stories. Our stories aren't just for our own benefit. We find the real power of our stories when we share them with other people.

Our stories connect us to other people. We find common ground in the beautiful and broken seasons alike. All who have experienced love, laughter, achievement or gratitude have also experienced their fair share of heartache, frustration, uncertainty or remorse. Pain doesn't discriminate based on background, status or religion. Even though your story is unique to you, the wisdom or perspective you have gained might be just what someone else needs. When we choose to include Christ in the stories we share, we have an incredible opportunity to present a faith that is not only relevant, but life-changing.

As we well know, being a Christian doesn't safeguard us from pain. We still struggle with insecurities and sin. But what sets us apart from the rest of the world is our trust that God is in control. It's our hope in Jesus Christ, who died for our sins that we may be reconciled with God. It's our belief that he's working all things out for our good and his glory. And it's our faith that, when our stories come to an end here on earth, a whole new story will be written—face to face with God himself—which will last for eternity. Our faith transforms the way we look at our circumstances. It is the root of our thankfulness in seasons of joy, and it is our source of strength to persevere through seasons of trial. All of life is an avenue for sharing your faith with others.

WHY I AM PASSIONATE ABOUT STORYTELLING

My passion for helping others share their stories started when I worked as program director for a high school youth group in Grand Rapids, Michigan. One of the core values of my ministry team was leadership development, both in the church and in the world. I noticed that the students who displayed the greatest leadership skills were the same ones who most actively pursued a relationship with Jesus. They read the Word on their own, they prayed, they asked hard questions. They did not compartmentalize their faith; in return, their faith gave them purpose, which they pursued wholeheartedly.

Desiring to see more of our students internalize their purpose as Christ-followers, I decided to plan a weekend retreat. The goal was to help our students make connections between their day-to-day life and their relationship with Jesus. The retreat was called, "Your Story Weekend," and it was broken down into two parts. The first portion focused on trust and openness. We completed a few exercises that challenged the students to be honest with each other about the difficult situations they faced. These conversations were powerful for the students. For many of them, it was the first time they had experienced such a level of authenticity in a church setting. The second half of the retreat focused on reconciling biblical truths with the difficult situations the students had shared. We encouraged them to look to God's character and the identity he had bestowed upon them as his children. Then the students spent time reflecting on patterns they'd seen between circumstances happening in their life and their relationship with God. By the end of the weekend, each student had the chance to share his or her story with the group. It was beautiful. The newfound confidence the students displayed was amazing. Recognizing that God was involved in their lives changed how the students saw themselves—which, in turn, transformed how they valued themselves. I saw firsthand the empowerment that comes through having confidence in one's self-worth and value.

Witnessing God move in my students that weekend spurred my desire to continue helping people discover their stories. In the summer of 2014, I married my husband, Trevor. He had started a doctoral program at the University of Arizona the year before, so shortly after our wedding, I moved down to Tucson, Arizona to be with him. Even though I was excited for the adventure of living in a new city with my new husband, the transition was really difficult. I felt out of place. I felt that opportunities to use my gifts had been taken away from me. And at times, I felt forgotten by God. Trevor's purpose in Tucson was obvious. But it was a long time before I found an outlet for my passion for storytelling. I always envisioned myself back in a youth ministry role, leading a group of students, like my role in Grand Rapids. But that opportunity never presented itself. So I kept praying and asking God, "What do you have for me here?" It happened slowly, but God started answering my prayers by giving me new, but scattered, ideas. Over a year later, those ideas finally morphed into something worth pursuing. Yep! You guessed it. That "something" was this book. My prayer throughout the writing process has been Psalms 115:1, "Not to us, Lord, not to us but to your name be the glory, because of your love and faithfulness."[1]

I believe that finding a storyline is transformational when life feels chaotic. When we identify God's presence in our lives, we find freedom from our past, peace in the present and direction for our future. If we are willing, God can use our stories in mighty ways to minister to others. Because you're reading this book, that tells me you are ready to discover your story and are willing to share it with others. That makes me so excited!

WHAT TO EXPECT IN TELL IT WELL

I wrote *Tell It Well* to help people discover the purpose in their stories. They are an avenue for sharing the gospel and God's overarching plan for redemption. Throughout this book, you will be encouraged to dig into your own story, ask God big questions and wrestle through them with him. We are in for an adventure together as we search for meaning, truth and purpose in the ups and downs of life.

Tell It Well is separated into three different sections. The first section, **"Discover Your Story,"** uncovers why your story is important and how to identify what your story is. It is primarily devotional and reflective. You will be given tools and prompts to reflect on your life and the ways God has worked in your life. I believe that God will speak to you in powerful ways as you work through this section. You will gain the ability to identify and articulate the things you've experienced and the things you've learned about God—it will be a game-changer. You will be able to identify specific ways God is working in you and through you, and you will learn how to connect the dots to form a cohesive story.

The second section is **"Own Your Story."** It is a charge and encouragement to own your story and entrust it to the Lord. It will help guide you to find God's presence in your life and live fully in your purpose going forward. You will identify ways to express the gospel through your own experiences, so that you can share the hope you have with others in an authentic and conversational way that doesn't come off as one-sided preaching.

The third and final section is called **"Share Your Story."** It focuses on helping you overcome the barriers that tend to keep us from opening up about our stories and relationship with God. This is where we will discuss the nuts and bolts of how to share your story in conversation. We'll answer questions like, "How do I empathize with people I don't feel like I relate to?" "Who can I trust with my story?" and "How much should I share?" I also share ways to bring God into your conversations and explain what Jesus has done for you in an understandable, relatable way. Really, it is a sendoff—a reminder that you are *already* equipped with everything you need to bring the gospel to the corners of the earth, as well as to your next-door neighbor.

THANK YOU FOR VALUING YOUR STORY

I'm thrilled that you decided to embark on this journey to better understand your story and use it to share hope with our hurting world. I have been praying for everyone whose eyes will read this book. I trust that the Lord will reveal himself to you in deep, lasting ways. We serve a good Father, and he is committed to making us more like him. I hope that as you read, you will be reminded of all his grace.

Reflection Questions

1. What comes to your mind when you think of explaining your faith to others?

2. What positive experiences have you had talking about faith or religion with others? What made them positive? What did you learn from these experiences?

3. What negative experiences have you had talking about faith or religion with others? What made them negative? What did you learn from these experiences?

4. How does the idea of using storytelling to explain your faith compare to other methods of evangelism you're familiar with?

5. How do you want to grow in your understanding of God and your personal story?

CHAPTER TWO

Why Your Story is Important

Sharing our stories is vulnerable. But that vulnerability is exactly what gives our stories the potential to be so powerful. There is a strong desire for authenticity in today's culture. We want to be known. We want others to be "real" with us. We want to go beyond simple niceties and small talk. Yet, though we crave it, sharing our stories and having conversations about faith is difficult. We question our relevance. We doubt our ability to answer questions that might be asked. We worry about misunderstandings or rejection.

Our culture is resistant of anything motivated by religion. We live in a time when fears are high, judgements are quick and opinions are polarized. Religious extremism is a terrifying reality across multiple religions, and we have seen the destruction it can cause. Many are left skeptical and distrusting of religion, and others are left cautious of stirring the tension. When everyone has their own interpretation of what warrants extremism, it can be difficult to navigate conversations about faith, much less start them. In a national Barna Group survey conducted in August 2015, researchers asked Americans to rate which religious actions or attitudes they felt were "extreme." The respondents who identified as having "No Faith" (Atheists, Agnostics, or Religiously Unaffiliated), overwhelmingly considered actions and attitudes with direct ties to politics as extreme. For example, 60% of No Faith respondents think that protesting government policies that conflict with a person's religion is extreme. 89% agree that refusing to serve someone because of their lifestyle conflicts with the vendor's beliefs is extreme. 73% believe that demonstrating outside an organization that a person considers immoral is extreme.[1] Strong reactions are to be expected in the political arena. But we see a similar pattern in the larger narrative of American religion, not only in politics.

In the same study, Barna continued to question society's perception of religion. One of the probes asked if participants agreed with the statement, "Christianity is extremist." 45% of No Faith respondents agreed.[2] That's a startling number, isn't it? If you're like me, your initial response to that number may be defensive. Maybe you blame the media for its poor depiction of Christianity in recent years, or dissociate yourself from "rogue" Christian sects. *It's not fair,* you may be thinking. *That's such a narrow, stereotyped view of Christianity. We're not all extreme—I'm not extreme.* But instead of pointing fingers, let's take the time to notice just how universal those feelings may be. Could the frustrating feeling of being pigeonholed be exactly how people outside of the faith feel when we define them based on their religious status? The best way to change any negative perception of Christianity is to know who holds these perceptions and seek to understand their perspective.

Taylor, a friend of mine who identifies herself as being non-religious, recently told me about the hurt she has experienced from Christians. She explained that often, when she meets Christians, they get along great—until they find out she isn't a Christian herself. Then the relationship changes. She mentioned the emphasis some Christians have placed on trying to "convert" her. When it didn't work, the friendship often came to an end. She told me, "How would it feel for them if I just assumed that they were non-religious like me, and talked to them as such? How it would feel for them if, upon finding out that they were religious, I tried to make them a non-believer like myself?" That would hurt, wouldn't it? After a while, it would be hard to trust a group of people who claimed to love you, but only seemed interested in changing your mind.

When we engage in conversations about religion and beliefs, we need to keep our motivation in check. This means investing in relationships with those of different faiths because we *love* them, because we want to *understand* them—not because they are a project. Approaching relationships with the main goal of conversion is dehumanizing. In effect, it says, "You are worth less because you don't share my belief." Of course, we want others to find hope in Jesus, but when our focus is only on *if* or *if not* they share our beliefs, we lose track of the individual's inherent value and beauty.

This is not a new problem. It is the same behavior demonstrated by the Pharisees in Matthew 9, which Jesus disrupted and condemned. Instead of judging people based on their current status, Jesus modeled how to love, serve and invite people into the fold of his mercy with compassion and grace. Jesus' style of love and relationship is attractive. Conversely, the opposite—using relationships as a means to an end—is ugly. When conversion alone motivates a relationship, it can't be masked. People notice and turn away. In fact, the attitude and action of trying "to convert others to one's faith" is seen as the third most extreme action by Christians, according to the Barna study. 83% percent of those with no faith are in agreement.[3]

Certainly not all Christians behave in this way. In reality, these descriptions represent only a minority. But we can't be naïve in thinking that we'll be exempt from another's assumption that if we start talking about faith, we are solely trying to convert them. If our goal is to engage in open conversations about faith—conversations that supersede narrow stereotypes—we'll need to do the work of building trust. One of the most practical ways we can do this is by inviting people with different beliefs to share their journey and perspective. When we willingly listen without judgement, we allow room for mutual respect and meaningful connection. Listening well can bridge the gap of preconceived stereotypes and create a space where authenticity is possible. Authenticity builds trust, and trust gives us the credibility to share our own story and reasons for belief in Christ.

Taylor is a great example of someone who seeks to understand each person as an individual, who values each person's story and personal beliefs. Despite her negative experiences with Christians in the past, she is always willing to give the benefit of the doubt and see people for who they truly are. At the end of our discussion she told me, "Even though my early life was colored by unfortunate experiences with select individuals, I don't hold any hate in my heart towards Christians. Almost all of my favorite people in my life are good Christians who let their faith guide them in very positive ways." I'm so grateful Taylor shared that with me. It fills me with hope. When we follow Christ well and treat others the way Jesus treated them, we can create and maintain meaningful relationships with people of all backgrounds. We can share our stories confidently, inviting others to see how we experience God. At the same time, we can love people with stories much different than our own and respect the conclusions they have come to.

Through practicing this myself, I have found that most people are open to talking about their religious beliefs or non-beliefs. The key to having open conversations is to root them in understanding and common ground. For people who grew up with a church background that emphasized apologetics, this may be a new approach for you. Apologetics, by definition, is a "systematic argumentative discourse in defense."[4]   When you enter a conversation with an apologetics mindset, you are ready to argue, defend, prove others wrong and debate. Think about it. How would you feel if you were on the receiving end of that kind of language? Would it make you want to open up and participate in a conversation? Probably not. That's not to say we can't disagree in a conversation rooted in understanding. Rather, finding common ground means choosing to respect the beliefs and conclusions others have come to, *while at the same time* maintaining peaceful confidence in our own. The difference is in our approach to these conversations, not the strength of our beliefs.

Because religion and faith are deeply personal matters, it is silly to think that a strong argument alone could be enough to change someone's belief. And to think that *we* are the ones who can change someone's beliefs is even sillier. That's God's job, which Jesus made clear when he told the Jews, "No one can come to Me unless the Father who sent Me draws him."[5] And it is the Holy Spirit who beckons hearts and reveals the mystery of Christ: "For God who said, 'Let light shine out of darkness,' has shone in our hearts to give the light of the knowledge of God's glory in the face of Jesus Christ."[6] Our role is not to convict hearts, but to represent a faith that changes lives. Since we can't change minds or hearts, the best thing we can do is live and share our stories in a way that causes others to ask questions about God.

That is why story can be so powerful. It takes theology and makes it personal. It makes age-old traditions and texts relevant. Our stories bear witness to the reality that Jesus is alive and his presence in us makes a difference. We see evidence of this today. Among Millennials, personal testimony is the leading catalyst for people to make the decision to follow Christ. In 2014, the Barna Group conducted yet another study on the religious landscape of America. Their goal was to trace any changing trends amongst Americans in regards to their involvement in, or perceptions of, religion in America. One thing that the study found was that nearly 40% of Millennials identified as "having no religion."[7]

Nearly all of these "no religion" Millennials also reported having a Christian background or previous experience with Christianity. So these aren't cases in which they have never heard the gospel or are "unreached." Rather, it means that they have seen a representation of Christianity and rejected it. Many Millennials believe they understand what Christianity is all about, but they have decided it's not for them. This mindset is our greatest obstacle. But the good news is, it just might also be our greatest strength. Researchers analyzing Millennials' perceptions of the Christian church found that 70% of Millennials who *had* converted to Christianity (from a different religion or from no religion) converted because of the impact another person had on them. It was relationship, and the connection of a personal testimony, that catalyzed their own decision to follow Christ.[8]

I was intrigued by this research, so I decided to conduct a survey of my own. I asked people to describe their hesitations about bringing up faith in their conversations. Overwhelmingly, the Christians who responded answered with some variation of, "I'm afraid that other people won't want to listen to me if I talk about religion," or, "I'm afraid I will shut the conversation down." However, the majority of non-Christians who responded said things like, "I enjoy philosophical discussions and challenging my beliefs," or, "Having religious discussions doesn't threaten anyone's beliefs." I found this so interesting and heartbreaking.

The patterns I noticed in my survey were confirmed in the data Barna collected in their 2015 national poll. Barna asked, "Which groups do you think it would be difficult for you to have a natural and normal conversation with? Mark all that apply." Sadly, Evangelicals reported the most groups (people with different religious beliefs or lifestyles) with whom it would be difficult to have normal conversations. And the numbers were staggeringly high. 87% of Evangelicals noted that they thought it would be difficult for them to have normal conversations with Muslims or members of the LGBT community. And 85% said it would be difficult to have conversations with Atheists. These perceptions were not reciprocated. Only 66% of Atheists reported the same conversational difficulty towards the evangelical group.[9] David Kinnaman and Gabe Lyons addressed this survey in their book, *Good Faith*, with a statement I couldn't agree with more: "If Christians are to be agents of good faith, we've got to overcome the real or perceived barriers of talking with people who don't already agree with us. We need to become experts at engaging in difficult conversations."[10]

If you fall into the 85% of Christians who worry about having conversations with atheists or non-religious people—take a deep breath. You can overcome the fears that hold you back, and you can find meaningful ways to find common ground with people who hold different beliefs. Your story can help you meet others where they are. It empowers you to connect with others and speak truth into the areas of life where they need it most. There will be times when you doubt this, and there will be lies telling you differently. When they come, be brave and remind yourself of the truth. You are important. Your story is important. *Your story is worth sharing.* And no matter where your journey takes you, God will never leave you or forsake you.[11]

What if, through your story, someone else came to know Jesus? What if, through your story, someone was able to see the light at the end of the tunnel? What if, through your story, someone was finally able let go of the shame they've been holding onto for so long? Would you share it? I hope so!

Maybe you are excited to share your story and talk about faith with others, but you just don't know how to start the conversation. Or maybe you still aren't sure what your story is, or how to identify God's work in your life. Wherever you fall on the spectrum, you are in good company. Together, we will walk through the steps of identifying our stories and engaging in conversations about life, faith and religion well. In order to do this, we need to dispel some of the confusions and misunderstandings about what it means to share our stories.

Reflection Questions

1. How do you see stereotypes affecting your ability to connect or have conversations with people of different backgrounds and beliefs?

2. Why do you think there is such a trend for Millennials to opt out of religious affiliation? What factors do you think influence that trend?

3. Is there a group of people you feel uncomfortable talking with? What makes you uncomfortable?

4. How do you think your personal story could impact someone else?

CHAPTER THREE

Common Misconceptions About Sharing Your Story

"For I am not ashamed of the gospel, for it is God's power for salvation to everyone who believes, first to the Jew, and also to the Greek." -Romans 1:16

For those of you who grew up in the church, any doubts and confusions about sharing your stories may be intensified. Maybe you've heard testimonies from a stage that sounded more like laundry lists of past sins, rather than celebrations of a gospel of hope and redemption. Maybe you were taught to evangelize to others using a three-step tract, but you just can't reconcile that approach with your sincere love for your friends. Maybe those tactics felt too cold, like pushing an agenda rather than meeting people at their deepest need. Or maybe the idea of sharing your story feels like too much pressure because you just can't make sense of your story.

You want to represent God well, but your life feels chaotic. You aren't sure how God fits into the picture. You may be wondering, *How could my story be a beacon of God's hope?*

When I asked people to tell me about their experiences with talking about faith in conversation, I also asked them to describe their feelings associated with sharing their stories. Most people explained it wasn't something they felt comfortable doing because they had so many fears, confusions and doubts. The most frequently stated sentiments included:

- I'm afraid people will judge me.

- I'm afraid of letting others see my flaws and vulnerabilities.

- I'm afraid I won't be able to explain my beliefs.

- I'm afraid I won't be able to relate with people who have different religious backgrounds.

These fears are understandable. The idea of "sharing your story" sometimes feels like a pressure to share deep, dark secrets, which is not appealing. Rejection, judgement and condemnation are experiences we naturally try to avoid. But the fear of these experiences keeps us small and ineffective in our witness. Fear is a trap that comes from Satan, who wants to keep you quiet and stuck in shame. I've discovered that choosing to share your story is a celebration of the freedom you've found in Christ. Telling others about the ways you have experienced God's presence in your life triumphs over Satan. It smashes fear in the face. It allows you to taste the fullness of joy that comes from acknowledging that God loves you, takes care of you and calls you higher. This does not guarantee that you will completely avoid rejection, judgement or condemnation when sharing your story. It may happen from time to time. But my hope for you is that you reconsider how much credence you give the fears that tell you to stay quiet. Don't let yourself be governed by fears, lies or shame. Life is too short!

When fears or hesitations arise, we need to examine them. It is important that we confront our fears and deal with them directly. Pretending they don't exist will only lead to further confusion down the road. One of the fears I struggle with most frequently is, *I don't have anything unique to say. Why would they listen to me?* You may find that ironic. The girl who says you have a story worth sharing consistently doubts that she has something worth saying. And while those statements may be contradictory, I know the two go hand-in-hand. Wrestling with that deep-seated fear in my personal life has opened my eyes to the contrast between allowing fear to rule and walking in Christ's abundant freedom. God gave me life, he gave me purpose, and he gave me a story. *I have something to say, and my story is worth sharing*—just as yours is, too.

When we notice that fear is holding us back, we need to pray and ask ourselves the following questions: *What am I afraid of, specifically? What is the worst-case scenario and how likely is it to happen? Is this a valid reason to not share my story? Is there a different way I can approach the conversation that would feel more comfortable?* When we take the time to step back and answer these questions objectively—instead of simply responding to our fear— we are able to determine the best way to approach each scenario. In this way, we can let go of our anxious thoughts, give them to the Lord and trust that he will give us understanding and wisdom. He will guard our hearts and minds in Christ Jesus.[1]

What I found most compelling about people's responses concerning fear was the words they used when they talked about story-sharing. I realized that for many, the concept feels vague, yet they also sense that there is a "right" way to share your story. The combination of feeling like there is a right way to do something and not knowing what it is causes so much insecurity. As I explored these widespread insecurities, I discovered that there were several commonly-held misconceptions about what it means to share your story and how to do it well.

I have held many of these misconceptions myself, and I know that in order to be able to share our stories confidently, truthfully and in a way that honors God, we need to confront these misconceptions head on. So we're going to dive into the five most common misconceptions, dispel these myths, and reorient our ideas of what it means to share our story with others well.

MISCONCEPTION #1: YOUR STORY IS AN ACCOUNT OF ALL THE WAYS YOU'VE MESSED UP.

Have you ever been asked to share your story with a group of strangers? The first time I shared my story with a group of strangers was during my freshman year of college. I was on a mission trip with a handful of other young people, and we were sitting around a campfire. It was our first night together, and we were prompted to share our testimonies with each other. The goal was to quickly build trust and community within our group.

While my heart yearned for authentic relationships with that sort of transparency, I was still scared out of my mind to open my mouth. I didn't know how much I was supposed to say, or how to say it. That was uncomfortable enough in itself. But in addition, I had zero idea how the group would respond to me. My jaw clenched so tightly that my teeth began to ache.

One by one, the braver people in the group began opening up and sharing their stories with the group. Very quickly, the stories turned into long, detailed accounts about all the mistakes we had ever made: from the scars we'd had since childhood to the areas of life we were struggling with currently. A total bare-all—everything was exposed.

The special setting we were in turned out to be a safe place for people to open up. The group lovingly and compassionately responded to each other's stories. We understood each other better, and learned how to love and encourage one another where it really hit home. I am grateful for that experience, and how it impacted my life. But I am also conscious of the fact that at the time, I didn't feel like I had a choice to share or not to share. And that's why this misconception needs to be addressed right out of the gate. If the expectation is that "sharing your story" means telling all the ways you've messed up, or all the ways you've been hurt, it can be intimidating, confusing and even dangerous if taken out of the context of loving community.

Unfortunately, I think that's the image most people have in their heads when they think about sharing their stories: that the core of your story includes details about your mistakes, struggles and secrets. No wonder sharing our stories makes us so nervous!

There is a place for that kind of transparency in Christian community, but I don't believe it is necessary, nor appropriate, every time we share our stories. I can think of several times I've been in a church service or worship gathering where someone walked on stage to share their story, only to quickly divulge intimate details about their past relationships and sin. While speaking in front of a group of people is understandably overwhelming, it's also overwhelming for listeners to sift through so much delicate and heavy information. Oftentimes, emotions are stirred, but the message is obscured.

The decision to laundry-list our mistakes and letdowns happens so frequently because we simply aren't prepared to share our stories. So we default into saying what we think we're supposed to say, with a bit of personal spin. But this misses the point. When we have the opportunity to share our story with others, the goal is to point our audience to Christ. We want our stories to communicate how Jesus' love and forgiveness have set us free! Acknowledgement of our sin and depravity is essential when explaining our need for God's grace, but it doesn't require us to expose every detail.

By preparing beforehand and knowing your story, you will be able to share it well. The truth of the gospel will shine more brightly through your testimony. We need to use discretion with what we choose to share and with whom. When you have the opportunity to share your story, it is best to set boundaries ahead of time so that you don't over-share or distract those listening with an overwhelming amount of details. Having boundaries gives you control and command over your story. This doesn't mean you follow a script when sharing; rather, you know your story so well that you are able to adapt it to naturally fit any conversation.

Keep in mind, I am not talking about the conversations you may have with close friends, spouses or mentors as you walk through life and deal with difficult issues. I hope that you can dig in deep with your people and feel comfortable with transparency. I pray that you are able to work out your messy seasons with people who have proven their loyal willingness to hold you accountable. They can support you, encourage you and help you determine how to share those details in other settings.

Your story is so much more than the sin and pain that has marked your life. *You are a redeemed child of God.* There are so many people who need to hear *that* story. Embrace your identity and share it boldly. As you work through your story, I encourage you to go into the dark places of your past, as well as the areas of your life that you are struggling with today. It's important that we recognize those areas and all the feelings associated with them. Instead of leaving those memories in the dark and shutting them out, let's face them and find healing from them. Let's acknowledge the reality of our painful pasts and "turn on the lights." Once the lights are on, we are more equipped to share about those areas of life with grace and discernment.

It's possible to gain a new perspective on seasons of pain and darkness: a perspective that identifies God in the midst of all life's circumstances, and recognizes how he has used those situations for his glory and your good. When you have control over your story, you will be able to choose which seasons will be most helpful when you next have the opportunity. You will be able to use your story to point to Christ, without getting lost in the weeds of past regrets.

MISCONCEPTION #2: YOU NEED A CRAZY STORY IN ORDER TO EFFECTIVELY SHARE THE GOSPEL.

God places us in the situations he deems best, and then saves those he calls in the way he deems best. He uniquely knows the way to our hearts, by attracting our attention in the exact moment when our hearts will be open and receptive to him. This is amazing, awe-inspiring and really difficult for me to wrap my head around. How does he know us so well? Our inability to comprehend the ways of God is a prompt for us to direct all the glory to him. And after all, that's what sharing our stories is all about, right?

All Christians have this story in common: we are saved by God's grace. We, who were once dead in our sin, are made clean and brought back to life. We are covered by grace through the blood of Jesus Christ, and we now have eternal life. We are adopted. We are set free. We are loved. This story is amazing—and it is always amazing, no matter the context. It's amazing if you were once an atheist who one day recognized the presence of God, or if you have had a steady, sincere faith in God since childhood. No matter how God's work has played out in your life, you, as a Christian, have been saved from sin and death, and you get to live this life in the freedom of Christ. And when you pass away, you will spend eternity with God himself in heaven. No matter what your unique version of this story is, or how it is told, it is beautiful. Your story is powerful. There are people out there who need to hear you tell it.

To highlight this point, I asked two friends to briefly share with me how they came to know Jesus. Both of their stories are unique, but neither are particularly dramatic or crazy. Rather, they are examples of how God moves and speaks in many ways, but all give reason to praise his name.

ASHLEIGH'S STORY

My faith story is rooted in the power of "generational faith": Faith passed down from grandparents, to parents, to myself, with each generation deciding to grasp hold of it individually, and furthermore, teaching and molding their children in God's grace. I share this so that those who either grew up in the church and/or a Christian home understand that generational faith is good. It is something to strive for. It does not water down Christ's redeeming gospel, but rather, gives hope to each generation and helps to continually fulfill the Great Commission, that all people have the opportunity to hear and to know the gospel so that they may believe. I am SO thankful for and blessed by my faith story.

ALYSSA'S STORY

Before I became a Christian, I thought that church was just a place where people went on Sundays. I thought it was boring, and definitely not for me. My interpretation of Christians was that they were nice, normal, giving, everyday people who believed in a God that I didn't understand. I was first attracted to the idea of Christianity when I saw a "spark" and "light" in other people who loved Jesus. I noticed something different about them, but I couldn't figure out exactly what it was. I wanted to figure out what that "spark" was because I wanted something to believe in for myself. I wanted hope for my life and for my future. I yearned to have faith in something, and I wanted to believe that there was a purpose for me here on earth. I decided to follow Jesus after eight years of conversations, mentorship, digging into my Bible, rollercoasters of ups and downs, and strong Christian friends to help me along the way. I accepted Christ on October 26, 2011. I was sitting on the living room floor in my first apartment, surrounded by my three amazing roommates and candles. It is a special moment I will never forget.

There's this notion that in order to share the gospel through your story, you need to have an out-of-control past—full of drugs, sex or near-death experiences—with a "spiritual" present, such as being a street pastor or worship leader. I have heard people use this misconception—that their story isn't "crazy" enough—so many times as an excuse not to share, and it saddens me. Many people believe, on some level, that in order for their story to make an impact or be meaningful to others, it needs to be dramatic. In fact, I think this is why over-focusing on hard times is so common when we do share. But what I don't think people realize is that when they discount the potential impact of their story, they not only relinquish the opportunity to share the gospel, but they also perpetuate this message: If my story isn't "good enough" to share, yours might not be either.

Several other problems stem from this misconception. First of all, we need to be careful about how our desire for a thrilling story may affect our brothers and sisters. For those who have lived "crazy" stories, the high drama can often overemphasize past sin or romanticize it in an unhealthy way. When these testimonies aren't told carefully, they can unintentionally spread the message that it's okay to do whatever you want while you're young, because God will forgive you later when you are ready to straighten up. We know this isn't biblical, as Paul addresses this exact sentiment in Romans 6: "What should we say then? Should we continue on in sin so that grace may multiply? Absolutely not! How can we who died to sin still live in it?"[2]

On the other hand, our brothers and sisters with less dramatic lives are left questioning if their stories will be useful for evangelism. They might feel disconnected from non-believers, or wonder if they will be taken seriously. What makes this misconception especially saddening is that it pits one Christian against another. A distorted competition arises out of who has the most rebellious or exciting story. This wrongly takes the glory away from God and places it on the person—or worse, the sin.

When we share our stories, or encourage others to, we must keep in check this temptation to compare. May we seek wisdom and purity to elevate Christ above all. What we all have in common as Christians is that we are all sinners, and we have all been redeemed by God's grace. He decides how to bring each of his children into the family. Instead of comparing with each other, we must simply celebrate each other and praise God for his fascinating creativity that he demonstrates within each of us.

MISCONCEPTION #3: YOU NEED TO UNDERSTAND COMPREHENSIVE THEOLOGY.

The thought of sharing the gospel makes many people nervous. It can feel like a lot of pressure. *What if I don't know how to explain it? What if they ask questions I can't answer? What is the gospel, anyways?* This concern tends to come from a sincere place in our hearts; we want to represent God well. However, our nervousness may warp into a dangerous misconception when we start believing that if we fumble, we somehow let God down.

A friend recently shared an analogy with me. I believe it paints a poignant picture of the truth we need to take hold of to fight this misconception. She told me to think about a loving dad with a little baby who is just learning to walk. The dad is so proud of his child each time she pulls herself up and stands for a couple seconds— even if she keeps falling down. He cheers her on, celebrates her and tells her how well she is doing. Even when she falls to the ground, her dad continues to cheer her on by reminding her of his love and how proud he is of her progress.

This dad doesn't see his daughter as failing to walk; rather, he sees her growth. He knows that she is getting stronger, developing coordination and learning to hold her own weight. Her dad is proud of her at every stage of learning, and he is always right there to hold her hands and help her.

That's a picture of our Father, friends. He is so proud of us when we step out and take risks in faith. You will not let him down when you stand up for truth but no one listens. He will not be disappointed if doctrine confuses you or you make a theological error. God will uphold you with His righteous right hand; we don't need to fear being without his counsel or his help.[3]

It's easy to work ourselves up and complicate the gospel. We often forget that the gospel can be summed up pretty simply in one of the most memorized Bible verses: "God so loved the world that he gave his one and only Son, that whoever believes in him should not perish but have eternal life."[4] That is the gospel. God loves us. We broke his heart by choosing sin over him, but he loves us so much that he sent Jesus to die in our place. He even did this while we were still sinners! And if we believe in Jesus, we are redeemed, set free and able to live for eternity with him in heaven. Hallelujah!

Of course, the details of the Christian faith are much more complex when we dive into them, but that is a good thing. When we talk about devoting our lives to something, we want that "something" to be substantial, profound and nuanced, right? Christianity is a deep and complex religion. Many hard questions are asked about religion, and these questions are often valid. *Why would a loving God let people go to hell? If God is so good, why does he allow so much suffering? If God is really in control, why hasn't he answered my prayers or changed my circumstances?* While the answers don't come easy, the Christian faith is sturdy and can provide answers. You don't need to have all the answers, but please don't shy away from such questions. In C.S. Lewis' book *Mere Christianity*, he writes that complexity actually indicates realness. The excerpt below encourages me to press into the complexities of God and the Christian faith. I hope it encourages you, as well:

> Very well then, atheism is too simple. And I will tell you another view that is also too simple. It is the view I call Christianity-and-water, the view which simply says there is a good God in Heaven and everything is all right—leaving out all the difficult and terrible doctrines about sin and hell and the devil, and the redemption. Both of these are boys' philosophies.

It's no good asking for a simple religion. After all, real things are not simple. They look simple, but they are not. The table I am sitting at looks simple: but ask a scientist to tell you what it is really made of—all about the atoms and how the light waves rebound from them and hit my eye and what they do to the optic nerve and what it does to my brain—and, of course, you find that what we call 'seeing a table' lands you in mysteries and complications which you can hardly get to the end of. A young child saying a child's prayer looks simple. And if you are content to stop there, well and good. But if you are not—and the modern world usually is not—if you want to go on and ask what is really happening—then you must be prepared for something difficult. If we ask for something more than simplicity, it is silly then to complain that the something more is not simple.[5]

The good news is that Christianity can stand up to the greatest skeptic. But the greater news? We don't need to have all the answers, or be the most eloquent speaker to share the gospel in a way that resonates. Let's not sell God short on his ability to change another person's life through a simple explanation of the gospel. Instead, let's trust in his Holy Spirit that is within us to give us the responses and wisdom we need when we find ourselves at a loss. A successful presentation of the gospel is one where you are speaking from a heart full of love and grace, simply sharing the difference that Jesus makes in your life. We don't need to have all the answers; we just need to be willing.

MISCONCEPTION #4: WE CAN SHARE THE GOSPEL WITHOUT USING WORDS.

There is a quote commonly attributed to St. Francis of Assisi that says, "Preach the Gospel at all times. Use words if necessary."[6]

This phrase has become popular in Christian culture today. I'm sure this quote has been shared with the best intentions in mind. I imagine people use it to encourage Christians to evaluate their actions and make sure they are reflecting Christ before they start telling others to follow him. It's a question of hypocrisy: *He can talk the talk, but can he walk the walk?* I wholeheartedly agree with the importance of our faith being authentic and displayed in our actions, instead of just our words. However, as the popularity of that mantra has spread, I believe an unintended interpretation has spread as well.

It seems that many latch onto the idea that preaching the gospel through their actions, but neglect the reality that in most cases, words *are* necessary. People aren't automatically going to know that you do what you do because of Jesus—there are plenty of nice, good-hearted people in the world who don't follow Jesus at all.

My friend Gabriel is a great example of someone who preaches the gospel both through his action and through his words. For the past year, Gabriel has woken up early every Saturday morning and heads to the kitchen. He pulls out stacks of tortillas and bags of cheese, and makes huge batches of refried beans. After he assembles all these together into breakfast burritos, he loads them into his car and drives to Santa Rita Park in downtown Tucson. Santa Rita Park is known to be a gathering place for much of Tucson's homeless population. He calls his ministry Blessed Beans, and let me just tell you—those beans are so blessed.

One weekend, I got to experience Blessed Beans with our church's youth group. Gabriel walked us through the whole process, from the burrito-making to engaging with the homeless at the park. When we pulled up, Gabriel opened up the trunk and invited over anyone interested in some breakfast. As people congregated, it was obvious that they knew Gabriel and that he had invested in relationships with them. He briefly explained why we were there and prayed a blessing over the people, the food and our time together. While we were at the park handing out burritos, Gabriel was far more focused on the people and their conversations than on how many burritos were being passed out. He was serving the homeless and meeting their need for food, but he knew their deepest needs were love, friendship and dignity—and he made those the priority.

I asked Gabriel for his thoughts on the mantra, "Preach the Gospel at all times. Use words if necessary." He answered:

I've heard that phrase quite a bit, and I don't agree with it entirely. Words must be spoken, or else no one will never know why we are doing good deeds in the first place. But from experience, presenting the gospel straight-up to complete strangers, or even to people you know, may cause them to disregard you immediately. Planting a seed with someone goes a long way. This means building a relationship with someone and having multiple conversations over time. Through time, trust is built, and that's when life experiences and testimonies are shared. I believe that the righteous acts we do in front of others are important as we follow Christ. But it's through simple conversation that we meet them where they're at.

Over the past couple of years, I've heard Christian friends, non-profits and outreach ministries incorporate the phrase, "Preach the Gospel at all times. Use words if necessary," into their explanations of why they interact with others the way they do, do the work they do or serve others the way they do. What I've noticed is that this phrase is often tacked on at the end, almost as if being offered as an excuse. I'm afraid it's become an easy cop-out from actually doing the real work of sharing the gospel.

Through Gabriel's work with Blessed Beans, everyone at Santa Rita Park knows why he is there. They know that he is a Christian, and that it is God's love moving through him that spurs him on to serve the homeless. We can learn from Gabriel's example. Everything we do should point to God, but we have a choice in how to use our words. The decision to share the gospel isn't a choice between "yes" or "no," but rather a question of *"How?"* Every person we interact with is different, and therefore we must be sensitive to the Holy Spirit's leading in our interactions with them. We should always be prepared to share the gospel with others, but sometimes starting with love and relationship-building is more of a testimony to God's love than directly preaching the gospel. In fact, this leads me to our final misconception.

MISCONCEPTION #5: SHARING THE GOSPEL MEANS PREACHING AT PEOPLE.

This misconception is so interesting to me because it's the biggest hesitation amongst both Christians and non-Christians. Non-Christians don't want to be preached at, and Christians don't want to come off as hard-handed, judgmental or insensitive. But there is good news. Preaching and talking naturally about your personal relationship with God are two very different things.

When I asked people to describe their biggest challenge when talking about God with others, many reported fear that mentioning their faith would bring up pre-conceived ideas about Christians. They felt like it would turn people off to anything else they have to say. *I don't want to be viewed as a "Bible-thumper". I don't want to make them uncomfortable. I'm afraid something I say will turn them off to the Gospel. I don't want them to feel judged.* These responses were common. The risk of rejection often seems too high because of these fears.

As I read these responses, I nodded my head in agreement. I get it. I struggle with these fears, too. I've had people shut down conversations as soon as I mentioned God or my faith, and it was awkward. But that was it. Life went on. Maybe you have experienced more intense reactions than mere awkwardness. But even so, I hope that, like me, you also have stories of being totally shocked by how receptive someone was to a conversation about God.

We can't control the thoughts people already have about God, but we can control how we bring God up in conversation—which just might let others see him in a new light. That's why we're focusing on using our personal stories as a way to share the gospel. It's a much different approach than coming at the conversation with the motive to "change their mind" or "make them see the truth." If we are willing to invite the name of God into our daily conversations, without the motive to preach at or convince other people that our beliefs are the right beliefs, we open up many more avenues for God's love to be shared with others.

Reflection Questions

1. Do any of the misconceptions outlined in this chapter sound similar to your own ideas about sharing your story? If so, which ones?

2. How were you challenged to look at your story differently by deconstructing these common misconceptions about story?

3. What is the next step you can take to overcome your barriers to sharing your story? What fears or insecurities might you need to give over to God?

4. How might you be misinterpreting the work God is doing in your life? What might it look like to share about your experiences with God? Pray and ask God to give you his grace and wisdom in every opportunity you have to share your story.

CHAPTER FOUR

Finding a Story in the Fog

Uncovering our stories can be hard work. It takes time, patience and intention. Oftentimes, identifying our stories feels like looking at a "Where's Waldo?" picture the size of a semi-truck. There are so many random pieces, so many distractions. How do we know where to start? How do we sort out the significant from the insignificant? Even if we have all the pieces, the task of putting them all together into a single storyline can be daunting.

I call this feeling "the fog." It's a feeling of disorientation and disarray. I visualize it as a broken compass, one that keeps spinning and shifting, unable to find north. Being in the fog feels unsettling. It makes us restless. It can be brutal. We tend to experience the fog when we go through transitions, as we realize that things aren't as simple as they once seemed. As I've gotten older, I've realized that I spend a lot more time in the fog than I do out of it. Interestingly enough, it doesn't seem to make a difference if the antecedent to a foggy season is good or bad. Learning to live in a new reality can be trying and tiring, even if we enter into it with excitement. Unfortunately, since the fog is essentially a process of learning and growing, there aren't any quick fixes for us to bypass it. But we can learn to recognize when we are in a foggy season. The ability to recognize the fog is a sign of maturity. How you choose to engage with the fog determines how you will benefit from it. I encourage you to use the fog as an opportunity for growth, and look for ways that this foggy season will tie into the grander story of your life.

The first time I realized I was in a fog, I was halfway through my freshman year of college. I had decided to leave the school I had been attending in Tennessee after one semester, and I had moved back home to Grand Rapids. I made the decision without a clear reason or explanation why, but I felt confident that the Lord had called me to do it. It was a rare and special moment in my life when I remember God speaking to me clearly. So I did it. I packed up and made the move.

It wasn't long after returning to Grand Rapids when doubts flooded in about whether I had made the right decision. Like most college freshmen, I was struggling trying to make sense of who I was. I was having a difficult time finding my identity in a year of so many transitions. The difficulty was intensified by my stubbornness and refusal to admit I was struggling. I had always prided myself on my confidence, being firm in my beliefs and having a plan of where I was going in life. Emotionally, I had always been tough and strong. I found it hard to ask for help or show weakness. And because of all of these characteristics, I kept pushing forward, afraid to acknowledge the struggle inside of me.

The problem had started long before returning home. When I first started school in Tennessee, I found myself in a cycle of uncontrolled binge-eating and making myself throw up. I was really disturbed by my actions, and by how quickly they became habitual. I'd like to say that I immediately thought to explore what was going on in my heart, but that didn't happen for me quickly. Instead, I did everything in my power I could think of to control the situation. I searched online to find an answer for what was happening to me. I made strict rules about what, when and where I could eat, in a fruitless attempt to prevent a binge. But my rules seemed to have the opposite effect. The binges became more frequent the more I tried to control them. I was so out of touch with what was going on inside me emotionally that I never considered that I might have been trying to numb some pain or find a sort of control in my life. I decided to meet with a counselor at school, hopeful that she would help me figure out what was wrong and how to fix it.

I remember sitting there in her cozy office. She had lit a nice, cotton-smelling candle and offered me a cup of peppermint tea. While the space was inviting and the counselor was as gracious as could be, I still had my barriers up. I was there for a solution, not to investigate the problem. Right out of the gate, I told her that I was struggling with binge-eating and throwing up, and that I had come to her for help in finding a way to stop these patterns. She nodded understandingly, and asked me to tell her about my background and transition to school. I told her that my transition to school had been going great. I was having a good time, making friends, and didn't feel homesick like some of my friends. She asked me a few more questions about the transition, and I started to feel like it was a waste of time. I thought, *This is going nowhere. It was a stupid idea to come here in the first place. You'll figure it out on your own, Jenny.* I kept looking at the clock, anxiously waiting for my half-hour session to end.

Towards the end of our meeting, the counselor told me that it sounded like I was under a lot of stress. Her words shocked me. And my defiance came out full-force when I looked her in the eye and denied it: "No, I'm not. I don't get stressed." (Ha, ha.) She asked me to make another appointment at the desk on my way out. I did so, but I ended up canceling it at the last minute. Instead, I continued to put my body, mind and heart through the relentless cycle of disordered eating. I tried fasting, exercising and only eating "healthy" foods, but nothing seemed to help. I told only one friend, who attended school with me. Sometimes I would sleep over at her dorm if I was feeling especially tempted to binge and vomit. But most of the time, the compulsion overtook me so quickly that I didn't even feel like I was making the choice to give in or not—it just happened. I was scared, confused and started losing hope I would ever be able to quit the habit.

Even in my striving for control, God started drawing me closer to himself. The more times I failed, the quicker I learned to call on him. The more I called on him, the more I chose to rely on him. And slowly, with lots of pain, I grew humble. My heart became softer and more in tune with God's. I started to see clearly that something deeper was going on. Even when I felt afraid to dig into the unknown, I learned that I could trust God to lead me through it.

I recently pulled out the journal that I kept during that semester. I was amazed by how my entries changed over time. They started as lists of things *I* needed to do to solve my problem, but they slowly conformed to prayers of giving my heart to the Lord. What is especially beautiful to me about those prayers is that I have since seen God answer them in my life. Here is an excerpt from one entry:

October 21, 2010

Oh Jesus, I need you. I am so lost. I have wandered so far from you. I keep messing up and giving into sin. I feel so ashamed; it's hard to have hope.

Reminders:

"Nothing can separate, even if I run away. Your love never fails."

"There may be pain in the night, but joy comes in the morning. Your love never changes."

"You make all things work together for my good."[1]

God, help me to realize, in a way that changes my behavior, that you never change. That you never leave. That you see my every action, and that it breaks your heart when I abuse my body. Help me to put redemption into practice. I pray that you would radically change the way I view the power of your healing hand.

I ask that you give me strength and perseverance to search out your heart so that mine will conform to yours. I ask for self-control, and I ask that you would point out other areas in my life where my lack of self-control and my lack of trust in you are manifest. God, I want freedom from this. I know that you give freedom, and freedom can only be found in you. Guide me as I struggle through this.

I ask for forgiveness for trying to solve this problem with my own human power. Humble me, Lord. I know that no change is possible without you.

Earnest prayers like these filled the pages of the journals I kept for the next couple of years. My struggle with disordered eating was by no means a one-and-done deal. But is any struggle so easily solved? As time went on, I continued to struggle with controlling my eating habits, but I was still able to experience God working in my heart and in my life in beautiful ways. He taught me about his grace—how he is totally sufficient to cover all of my sins. He taught me that I am covered by the righteousness of Christ, and that God really does see me as his pure, holy daughter! These are amazing truths. And as I began to believe them, I also learned to walk in them.

There was never a definitive day or moment when I became free of my disordered eating. Rather, freedom is a choice that I need to make every single day—sometimes multiple times a day. These days, I'm much healthier emotionally, mentally and physically, so choosing freedom is easier. I am extremely grateful. It took a long process of healing, but the lessons I learned are invaluable. In particular, I learned that God is continually at work in me. Even when I can't see him, when I fail, when I fall on my face again and again, he makes me more beautiful. This is true for you, too. When we are in a tough season, the battle feels constant. The disappointment, heartbreak, temptation, confusion—whatever the difficulty may be, it feels as though it will never end. But God is the faithful one, and we can trust him to see us through—even when we don't see the end. In those times, it's our job to keep staking our hope in the solid truth of who God is and what he says about us. Every time we choose truth and choose freedom, we take another step forward. At some point, you'll look behind you and realize how far you've come. You'll be out of the fog, and you'll have a story to tell.

WHAT DO I DO WHILE I'M STILL IN THE FOG?

Let me go back to what I stated at the beginning of this chapter, that most of life tends to be made up of one type of fog or another. This is good news. Do you know why? Because when we are in the fog, full of questions and uncertainty, we gain an extra dose of grace and empathy towards others who walk through similar seasons. And that is powerful stuff! My friend Allie's story is a perfect example of how God can take ongoing struggles in the fog and transform them for his glory.

Allie is the founder behind Wonderfully Made, a non-profit organization that teaches girls about their worth and value. Wonderfully Made is based in California, but the ministry hosts conferences, Bible studies and college group chapters around the country. I learned about Allie and the Wonderfully Made ministry through her Bible study *Wonderfully Made: Becoming Who You Are in Christ*,[2] which I used with a couple of high school girls I was mentoring. The Bible study was powerful for us as we found ways to reclaim our worth and value as children of God, despite what culture told us was the source of our worth. Details of Allie's life were interspersed throughout the study, and I became very intrigued by her story. I wanted to know how she found healing from her struggles with identity, worth and disordered eating, and how she began helping other girls and women find their own healing.

Let's fast-forward a couple of years, to when Allie and I both ended up attending an event called Yellow Conference. I had hoped to connect with her there so I could learn more about her journey. Though our paths never crossed at the conference, we later ended up communicating via email. When I asked about her story, I expected her to describe some monumental event that had forever transformed the way she saw herself. I thought she must have experienced some special kind of healing miracle that made it easy for her to stand firm on the truth she shared with so many women. Instead, I learned that though Allie's difficulties were similar to mine, she didn't them as excuses. I realized that I had bought into the lie that I couldn't help others if I was still struggling myself. In doing so, I had closed myself off to the possibility of being used by God in deep ways. I then recognized that truth and encouragement come through much clearer when spoken by someone who is right there in the trenches with you. And for me, that realization transformed my view on sharing my own story and struggles, even when I'm still in the thick of the fog.

I think Allie's perspective can be powerful for you, too. I asked if I could share part of her story in this book, and she graciously accepted. Here is what Allie had to say about ministering and leading, even during the foggy seasons of life:

> *I have to start by saying that I'm still on my journey—I definitely haven't arrived. If I'm honest with you, I find myself in a season of struggle in regards to body image. I think sometimes we believe that if we're leading in ministry, we have to have it all together, that we can't be struggling ourselves. While I have experienced freedom in many areas of my life, there are others that still need deep healing. A constant theme of my story has been God stripping away areas in which I place too much of my worth and identity. This process has been difficult, humbling and, at times, painful. But the beauty is that, as I free myself from the illusion of someone who has it "all together," I discover that in Christ alone, I am enough.*

> *I think that the lies I once believed about myself ran so deep that when I heard God's truth, I immediately clung to it and fought to make it manifest in my life. I couldn't keep to myself*

the truths that set me free; I had to share them with other girls, knowing and believing they, too, could be transformed. Making it my purpose to share life-changing truths and dispel lies has helped me to stay grounded. This is my life's work because I desperately need it myself.

What might it look like if we made the brave choice and accepted our current place in our stories—confusion, insecurity and all? I believe we'd discover with new understanding just how capable God is, even as he works through us. Our stories during the fog are what connect us to others in real time. When we're in the wilderness, feeling lost or unsure, or when we feel numb or disconnected, it's tempting to hide from others or say that we're doing okay. But when we choose the vulnerability of sharing the reality of our struggles, barriers drop down. We communicate the value of all seasons and all stories, and we model the choice to seek God's wisdom in the hard times. At the same time, I want to remind you of the discussion on boundaries and trust we discussed in the last chapter. You need to determine if your discomfort in sharing your story is rooted in lies or wisdom. If your fear is based in lies about your worth or calling, fight to overcome those lies and dig into vulnerability with others. If your hesitation is rooted in wisdom, perhaps because you suspect untrustworthiness or manipulation, heed the caution and save that part of your story for another time or place.

If you find yourself in the fog, here are some suggestions to help you make sense of the story within it:

- **Ask questions.** Make a list of all the things you feel like you don't know, or you don't understand. When you know what you are looking for, it is amazing how much easier the answers are to find!

- **Listen to others.** What things are the people around you learning? What are they struggling to understand? How can you learn from them and their experiences? What do the people you look up to do when they feel lost or unsure?

- **Read the Word.** Even when you don't feel like it, or you don't feel like you're getting anything out of it, read the Bible. The Psalms are my go-to when I feel stuck or disoriented about where my life is headed. King David, the Psalmist, had a lot of ups and downs of his own, and I am always encouraged by how well his prayers resonate with me. The Psalms often help me find the words for my own prayers.

Even in the fog, we can still diligently engage in the real-world problems and dialogue around us. Ask questions, listen to others, read the Word and pay attention to what's going on in your life and around the world. And while you engage in the dialogue of life, you will grow and learn and change. Change may not happen in a single moment, conversation or event. But you'll look back one day and, lo and behold, you'll realize that you are out of the fog.

Understanding your story isn't about fitting every piece together in a perfect sequence or knowing all the why's and how's of your experiences. Understanding your story is more about identifying long-term themes, periods of growth and pivotal moments that have played an important role in your life. We may never be able to see the full picture, and we might not have all of the answers to the questions in our story. But by piecing a story together, we are able to find deeper meaning in our life's journey and discover that our experiences provide opportunities to connect with others.

Reflection Questions

1. When have you found yourself in "the fog"? What was going on in your life at the time?

2. How do you react when you can't see the purpose in your current circumstances?

3. What are some ways that your beliefs about your self-worth affect your willingness to share your story?

4. What is the next step you can take to press into a foggy and unsure situation? Ask the Lord to guide you towards healing and wholeness in your story. Ask him to increase your trust and faith in his plans for you, even when you can't understand what he is doing.

CHAPTER FIVE

Embracing My Story

I started my blog, Jenuine Life, in August of 2013.[1] I was filled with hope, passion and mission. I wanted to explore the topic of beauty in a new way. My hope was to encourage women to look beyond physical appearance and identify beauty in themselves and others. My inspiration came from several sources, but mostly curiosity. I often heard people say phrases like, "It's what on the inside that counts," "Your beauty is within you," or, "She has a beautiful personality." While I agreed, and still do, that our "insides" are most important, I found those statements to be vague. How exactly does one nurture inner beauty? My goal in starting the blog was to create a community online where women would learn to identify tangible traits of beauty that come from within—courage, patience, resilience, joy, justice and vulnerability, for example. I believe that when you are able to recognize these characteristics, you are empowered to develop them in yourself. Additionally, you are enabled to speak specific encouragement to others. The more we acknowledge beauty, the more it grows.

Beauty is a topic that all women confront in an intimate way. Beauty is nuanced, and its pursuit is even more so. Beauty takes form in so many ways. Whether in the form of body shape, genuine laughter, intelligence, tenderness or creativity, all beauty stems from Christ. While beauty is diverse in nature, our culture has tried to simplify it, resulting in a very narrow standard of beauty that is all physical and certainly not universal. It can be challenging for women to remain steady and confident in the ebb and flow of inevitable body changes and cultural beauty standards. One way we can grow in our inner beauty is to find what inspires us, and then invest in those things. In doing so, we develop our identity. The more confident we are in our identity, the more Christ shines through. I believe there will always be tension between physical beauty and heart beauty, but I don't think we need to give up one to have the other. Rather, there is room to grow in our conversations about beauty, especially within the church subculture.

QUESTIONING BEAUTY

Beauty has been a consistent theme in my life and relationship with God. I've had ups and downs as I've learned about beauty. I've been on the hunt to find the meaning of the true beauty that God intends for us. I still have a lot of work to do in this area, but it has already been quite the journey.

Growing up, I heard plenty of teachings on modesty from the church. I was told to seek beauty in my heart, not my outward appearance. Real beauty, they said, was in the heart. While real beauty *is* found in the heart, the message confused me. Recognition of physical beauty was completely absent, almost as if it didn't exist. I internalized the message that any attention towards my body was a failure on my part—either I had either erroneously drawn the attention upon myself, or my heart wasn't beautiful enough to overshadow my body. I struggled to walk the thin line between confidence and pride, self-care and vanity. I wanted to be beautiful, as all women do, but at the same time, I felt shame for that desire. I also felt guilty if I was ever complimented for my appearance.

During my senior year of high school, I was voted "best-looking" by my class in a mock election. That experience made me face head-on my contradicting beliefs about beauty. Of course, the award was flattering, but inside myself, I wrestled with questions and feelings of shame. I certainly didn't think I was the best-looking girl in my class. I wondered how many others were now also walking around critiquing my face, hair and body. I felt like I had failed somehow. Was I really going to be remembered in the school yearbook only for my looks? My mind wandered to seeing my classmates at a ten- or fifteen-year reunion. What if I gained too much weight? What if I aged poorly? Would people judge me for years to come based on my appearance, instead of the person I had become?

Now that I am removed from the situation by several years, I understand that high school mock elections are just a drop in the ocean of high school memories. After graduation, I'm sure very few people can remember *who* was awarded *what*, unless they themselves had received the award. But what *is* important is how that experience wove itself into my self-concept. It handicapped me from seeing myself as a unified person. I felt like I was one-part body and one-part heart, but I couldn't figure out how to connect the two. So I began mistreating my body with the twisted hope that my heart would instead become the focus. In college, as my eating disorder continued, my concept of self and beauty further deteriorated. I knew that what I was doing was wrong, but I hated my body so much. I constantly critiqued myself, which heaped even more shame onto the self-hatred I held. I compared my body to every other woman's body around me. It was exhausting and isolating.

My sophomore year of college, I started to recognize that obsessing over my body—and all the problems I saw in it—was inhibiting my life. When I spent time with girlfriends, I was only half-there because my mind was consumed with comparison and self-doubt. When I was alone, my thoughts spiraled downward quickly. I knew that I needed to change my heart and self-talk, but I wasn't quite sure how. That's when I really began asking broader questions about beauty. *What is real beauty? Where does beauty come from? How can I cultivate beauty? How do I talk about beauty?* I started praying over these questions as I struggled to answer them. I practiced the discipline of "taking every thought captive."[2] Every time I noticed myself using harsh self-talk or comparing my body to someone else's, I asked God for forgiveness, and asked him to renew my mind. This was a very humbling process; it's outrageous how many times a day I needed to ask for forgiveness and a renewed mind.

As the days, weeks and months went on, I began to see progress. Even though I felt slow to learn, it is evident now that God was at work in my heart and in my life. It was so hard for me to accept God's grace for the mistakes I continued to make. In my head, I knew he had forgiven me, but in practice, I just couldn't believe it. I felt like I was nudging the limit of how many times God would forgive me for the same sin. My slowness to accept God's grace came from a place of fear and doubt. I was afraid to accept

God's forgiveness and the freedom found in it. I feared slipping back into the same sins, as though my failure could somehow disprove God's power—maybe even his existence. St Augustine eloquently describes a similar doubt in his book *Confessions*, as he contemplates the faith needed to accept grace and, ultimately, healing. He writes,

> But just as commonly happens that a person who has experienced a bad physician is afraid of entrusting himself to a good one, so it was with the health of my soul. While it could not be healed except by believing, it was refusing to be healed for fear of believing what is false.[3]

I wanted healing, and I wanted freedom. In a heap of tears on my dorm room floor, I told God I'd trust him. The sweetness of God's grace astounded me. I felt his love for me, even when I was still so messy. Since then, my knowledge of God's inexhaustible grace and forgiveness has become bona fide belief. But what has really surprised me is that God's grace doesn't only cover us after a sinful choice or mistake. Instead, God's grace is a gift we are given to live in at all times. It's his grace that protects us from choosing sin in the first place, and it's his grace that gives us strength to stand against temptation. His grace lets us see the world with a bigger perspective than the here-and-now. Accepting God's grace changes everything. If you are in a season of struggling with a pattern of sin and repentance, take heart. Even when it hurts in deep ways, this struggle forges a dependency on God that will pay dividends tenfold down the road. Keep going to God and asking for forgiveness—his grace won't run out. You can trust him on that.

EXTENDING GRACE TO OURSELVES

"Cheap grace is the grace we bestow on ourselves. Cheap grace is the preaching of forgiveness without requiring repentance… Cheap grace is grace without discipleship, grace without the cross, grace without Jesus Christ, living and incarnate." — *Dietrich Bonhoeffer[4]*

Why is it so hard to extend grace to ourselves? I've battled with this question a long time. The best answer I've come up with is this: control. We want to be the ones in control. We want the security of knowing that we can fix our own messes, that we can be "good enough" on our own. We want to be self-sufficient. Meanwhile, we also want justice, so we tend to make ourselves "pay" for our mistakes. This is how the cycle of shame starts. We hold ourselves to expectations we can't possibly achieve, we inevitably fail, and then we punish ourselves and raise the stakes for next time.

If you are stuck in a shame cycle, your thoughts might sound similar to these: "*I* am the problem," or, "*I* will never be good enough." Shame like this can be debilitating and isolating, which makes it a cycle. When we doubt ourselves or withdraw from people, we give the soundtrack of shame clearance to play as loudly as it wants. And if you let it, that shame soundtrack will play loudly, on repeat.

But those thoughts? The ones telling you that *you* are the problem? They are lies. When we choose to entertain them and even believe them, we choose Satan's lies over God's truth. Once the shame cycle starts, we fear exposing ourselves to the ones we love, and even to Jesus. Shame tells us to keep it all inside, in a dark corner where we can conceal our weaknesses.

"Then I heard a loud voice in heaven say: The salvation and the power and the kingdom of our God and the authority of His Messiah have now come, because the accuser of our brothers has been thrown out: the one who accuses them before our God day and night. They conquered him by the blood of the Lamb and the word of their testimony, for they did not love their lives in the face of death." - Revelation 12:10-11

How beautiful is that promise in Revelation 12:11? We are told that we overcome the accuser by the blood of the Lamb *and* by the word of our testimony. That means that sharing our story is a vital part to the healing journey as we overcome shame in our lives. It's an important part of learning to extend grace to ourselves, too. The key in verse 11 is the phrase, "for they did not love their lives in the face of death." We share the testimony of our lives because we seek to bring greater glory to the Lord, not to ourselves. We boldly proclaim Christ and his redemptive power in our lives. We trust the story he is writing for our lives, instead of the one we would write for ourselves.

It's hard for us to extend grace to ourselves because when we disappoint ourselves, we tend to keep score. Grace doesn't make sense on a scoreboard. But that's exactly the point: grace doesn't keep score. When we struggle with lies about our self-worth, it's important that we remember what is true about God and his character. He forgives us and welcomes us back with arms wide-open—even when we've made terrible mistakes. We do not need to fear approaching Jesus. Remember where he's sitting? On the throne of grace. Once we have accepted Jesus Christ as our Savior, we are cleansed by his blood. We are ransomed. We are redeemed.

"For we do not have a high priest who is unable to sympathize with our weaknesses, but One who has been tested in every way as we are, yet without sin. Therefore, let us approach the throne of grace with boldness, so that we may receive mercy and find grace to help us at the proper time." - Hebrews 4:15- 16

If we want to enjoy the riches of God's grace, we need to follow his lead and forgive ourselves as he has already forgiven us.

EMBRACING OUR STORIES, AND HELPING OTHERS TO EMBRACE THEIR OWN

Accepting God's grace transformed the way I saw myself. But it also changed how I saw others. I learned to see beyond my own circumstances, which made me more sensitive to the people around me. I realized that the comparisons I had been making between myself and other women didn't just hurt me, but harmed them, as well. Think about a time you caught someone sizing you up. It's a horrible feeling, right? It can be especially damaging if your confidence is already shaky. It can be a direct push into the cycle of self-shaming. The last thing I wanted was to be that "someone," pushing others into the shame cycle that I was trying so hard to climb out of myself. I needed to stop the comparison game—which required a lesson in confidence.

As part of that learning process, I paid close attention to women around me who exemplified confidence. The two traits I identified consistently in confident women were an outward focus towards others and an ability to be present in the moment. I noticed that these women seemed more concerned with the people around them than with themselves. I think this is what some people describe as "being comfortable in your own skin." Logically, if you aren't distracted by thoughts about your skin (or weight, hair, status, etc.), you are going to feel more comfortable and at ease. I observed women who displayed these traits and learned from them. With closer female friends, I took my observation a step further and asked them to share about their journey of achieving self-confidence. I learned so much from them, but most importantly, I learned that I was not alone in my struggles with body image and insecurity. While my personal experience was unique, the differences between me and these confident women were slight. The main difference was that they had resolved to not allow their insecurities to rule.

Realizing that I had a choice about what would define me liberated me from the cycle of shame I had been stuck in. I painted a big sign that read, "I am completely covered by grace. I am set free." I hung it on the wall across from my bed. It became the mantra I repeated to myself, over and over again. As the truth of God's grace seeped into my life, I grew passionate about helping others identify God's grace in their own lives. That's when I had the inspiration to start my blog, Jenuine Life. I chose to write my blog posts in the format of interviews. This allowed me to practice helping the women I interviewed to articulate their own stories, while also finding the greater storylines in the words they shared. The blog now has many examples of incredible women who have chosen to embrace their stories and use them to encourage others. Some women have shared their struggles with singleness, failure or the death of loved ones. Others have shared stories about witnessing God's healing, conceiving after infertility or starting a child sponsorship program. One thing they *all* have in common is an awareness of God's grace. The stories are powerful because they acknowledge the reality that sometimes, life is hard and confusing, and sometimes we mess up over and over again, but God's love for us and his ability to use us for his glory never change. When we accept that as truth, then we can give grace to ourselves and embrace our own stories—wherever we may be. Embracing our stories is what enables us to communicate them with authenticity.

Reflection Questions

1. What questions or themes do you find coming up in your life again and again? How have these themes influenced your view of yourself? How have they influenced your view of God?

2. Are there any struggles in your life that you find hard to give over to God? What would it take for you to trust God with them?

3. Is there anything keeping you stuck in a cycle of shame? How can you extend grace to yourself? What do you need to forgive yourself for?

4. How do you think your struggles and shame could be used to help other people who may also be hurting?

Part Two

OWN YOUR
STORY

CHAPTER SIX

The Power of Looking Forward

Stories are ultimately about a journey. They're about the process of moving from point A to point B, and the experiences and transformations that take place along the way. Our lives are made up of thousands of stories that weave together into one greater story. My hope is that my story points clearly to God. How about yours?

One of the reasons I am passionate about storytelling is because it is essential to living life intentionally. When we are able to identify a common storyline in our lives, it brings everything into perspective. We are able to see the trajectory of our lives, and seek knowledge and wisdom accordingly. This helps us make decisions that align with where we hope to be—in one year from now, five years, twenty-five years and beyond.

In addition, our stories have an incredible ability to produce hope in our hearts. We are hard-wired to think in term of stories. Stories engage us when our minds look forward and ask the question, "What will happen next?" The same is true when we consider our personal stories—*we look forward.* We hope for what is to come. Reflecting on our stories can reassure us of God's provision, which encourages us to trust him going forward. We can find peace in our current situation and derive meaning from our circumstances because we know that God has led us to this point. We can trust that he will guide us through any trial. Understanding our past allows us to deal with it appropriately. In turn, we are freed up to live life intentionally and in line with the legacy we hope to leave behind.

The Bible encourages us several times to have an intentional, forward-thinking mindset in life. Let's look at these examples:

- "Therefore, with your minds ready for action, be serious and set your hope completely on the grace to be brought to you at the revelation of Jesus Christ." - 1 Peter 1:13

- "Pay close attention to your life and your teaching: persevere in these things, for by doing this you will save both yourself and your hearers." - 1 Timothy 4:16

- "But the one who looks intently into the perfect law of freedom and perseveres in it, and is not a forgetful hearer but one who does good works—this person will be blessed in what he does." - James 1:25

Take a moment to consider the exhortations in these verses. We are called to take our faith seriously *and* to rely on God's grace seriously. We are called to be thoughtful about our lives *and* careful with the stories and teachings we share. We are called to own our identity as free, forgiven children of God *and* walk boldly in that identity. How well does your life reflect these calls? Where might you be holding back out of fear or control? These questions are not intended to come across as hard-handed, but rather as an opportunity to stop, reflect and re-orient our hearts to God.

As we seek the Lord with all our hearts, we can trust that he will lead us step by step in the path he has designed specifically for us. After all, it was God who decided to save us in the first place, and we know that he always remains faithful to the work he starts.[1] From the moment we put our faith in Jesus, we were redeemed by his grace. We were set with the seal of the Holy Spirit—which is the down payment of our inheritance awaiting us in heaven.[2] We received freedom from sin the very moment we were saved, when God started the process of renewing us and making us more like himself.[3] He promised to bring us from glory to glory, which means continually making us more like Christ until the day we see him face to face as made-perfect beings. You can cling to these promises when your heart is heavy and needs hope.

> *"Now the Lord is the Spirit, and where the Spirit of the Lord is, there is freedom. We all, with unveiled faces, are looking as in a mirror at the glory of the Lord and are being transformed into the same image from glory to glory; this is from the Lord who is the Spirit."*
> *- 2 Corinthians 3:17-18*

HOW DO WE PRACTICE HOPE?

One of the most powerful ways we can learn to have hope is through others who demonstrate it for us. I've been blessed to have learned to hope through a long line of family, friends and mentors. Someone who has taught me much about developing hope is my mentor, Judy. Judy has been a big part of my spiritual walk since I was a freshman in high school. One year, we served together on a mission trip in Mexico. While there, Judy led a devotional with our group, focusing on how God is faithful to bring us from glory to glory, even when the process is painful and the circumstances are uncertain. She described a story from Hannah Hurnard's book, *Hinds' Feet on High Places*,[4] which is an allegory that illustrates the journey of becoming more like Christ through tribulation and trust. The main character is named Much Afraid. Another character, The Shepherd, calls Much Afraid to The Heights of The Kingdom of Love, but the way is grueling and uncertain. The Shepherd promises to give Much Afraid everything she needs to ascend the mountains to the High Places, but he also explains that he can't just carry her there; first, she needs to gain the strength she needs to walk in the High Places.

Years later, that story sticks with me as a great metaphor and lesson in hope. In fact, I asked Judy if she would be willing to share the story again, for you. Judy's story explains and displays hope, and also models how we can glean and apply wisdom from other's stories—even through the fictional story of Much Afraid. Judy shares:

> Have you ever read Romans 5:3-5? It says, "Suffering produces perseverance; perseverance, character; and character, hope."[5] Does that sound right to you? Read it again… Slowly.

> Now, I usually associate "hope" with other uplifting words like joy, love, peace or faith. Words that resound with comfort. I think of verses like 1 Corinthians 13:13: "And now these three remain: faith, hope and love. But the greatest of these is love."[6] So why, in Romans 5, is hope now stuck with words such as suffering, perseverance and character?

The first time I read Romans 5:3-5, I was looking for comfort and "warm-fuzzies." I read this passage twenty years ago, during an emotionally and physically devastating period of my life. I was desperate for hope. I was desperate to pick up the pieces of my broken heart and shattered expectations and to find a reason to endure the pain and sorrow. I remember thinking, "I trust you, Lord Jesus. Please speak your words and bring me hope." I opened up my Bible to the concordance in the back, and looked for references to the word "hope." As my tear-filled eyes scanned the column, Romans 5:4 jumped out at me. I quickly flipped to Romans and read: "... suffering produces perseverance; perseverance, character; and character, hope."

I was in disbelief. My mind raced: *This can't be right! My Bible must have a typo. Surely hope doesn't start with suffering. I don't have time for perseverance; I need hope now! What does my character have to do with hope from God?*

I set my New International Version Bible aside and checked my husband's Bible: same wording. There was no typo in mine after all. Then I thought, *Maybe something was lost in translation?* I looked up the King James Version of the same verse: "...tribulation worketh patience; and patience, experience and experience, hope."[7]

My heart sank—"tribulation" just sounded like a more formal version of suffering! Then it hit me. God must really mean for our hope to spring up from the soil of pain, suffering, sorrow and heartache. As the truth of this Scripture gripped me, new questions spun in my mind. I cried out to God: *What does this look like in real life? How do I apply these words to my broken heart? Am I the only one struggling with this?*

God promised to be near the brokenhearted, and that day he used the words of Hannah Hurnard as a balm to soothe me. Her book, *Hinds' Feet on High Places,* helped me to know that I wasn't alone in my sorrow. Someone else had walked a path of hurt, disappointment, and pain—and she was willing to tell me her story, to let me lean in and glean wisdom from her journey. Her name was Much Afraid, and like me, she desired to follow The Shepherd to the High Places of Love and belong to him. But also like me, she was afraid of the cost, afraid of the pain, afraid that things might not turn out the way she wanted if she followed The Shepherd.

The pain, cost and trouble that I experienced didn't surprise me. I knew that Jesus himself warned us that "in this world, you will have trouble,"[8] but what caught me by surprise was the depth of the pain and sorrow. It seemed to be a valley or pit too deep for me to climb out. But Much Afraid's example of trusting The Shepherd and following him to The High Places of Love, where she was known and loved more fully than she could imagine, gave me the courage to join her on a similar journey, no matter the cost.

The Shepherd chose two traveling companions for Much Afraid. At first, the sight of them terrified her, and she rebuffed their help. They were not the companions she would have chosen for herself. You see, her companions were called Sorrow and Suffering. When The Shepherd introduced her to them, she thought he was being cruel. The very thought of walking with Sorrow and Suffering voluntarily was unimaginable enough, but to take their hands and trust them to lead the way seemed utterly beyond her.

Yet, as Much Afraid grew to know The Shepherd more, she knew that she could trust him, and even trust his choice of companions. When she fully embraced Sorrow and Suffering, her journey completely changed—not that the physical demands of the journey changed, but what changed was her attitude and emotional response. The moment I read that Much Afraid took the hands of Sorrow and Suffering, allowing them to lead her and teach her, my own heart softened. My mind found peace as I embraced God's choices for me on my journey. My sorrow and my suffering weren't chosen by God to punish me, but to train me to trust him and follow him every step of my journey.

As I followed her story, I witnessed Much Afraid encounter obstacles and enemies. I saw her lean on Sorrow and Suffering to not only endure physical challenges and overcome emotional pitfalls, but to actually thrive and flourish. As she dodged insults and battled with her enemies— Pride, Resentment, Bitterness and Self-Pity—I found that her journey paralleled my own. When Much Afraid questioned The Shepherd (repeatedly!) because she felt misled by Sorrow and Suffering—trekking through The Desert, along the Shores of Loneliness, in the Forest of Danger and Tribulation and in the Valley of Loss—I heard the echo of my own voice, asking God about my own situation: *How much longer? Why does it have to be this way? This is too hard! When will you lead me away from this pain?*

Much Afraid's transparency in expressing her doubts inspired me to also bring my doubts into the open, where I could see them and deal with them directly. I found that my sorrow could help me to overcome my doubt, and I saw my faith increase. Like Much Afraid, I learned that every obstacle could be looked upon as another lovely opportunity. I also allowed The Shepherd to transform me—not just carry me through and over obstacles, but to actually *change* me. Finally, I could see that these obstacles were truly opportunities to grow in faith and become more like the image of Christ. The saying "Attitude is everything" certainly applied in this case, but my growth was due to far more than an attitude adjustment.

You can't simply choose to change your attitude and be transformed into a new creation. No amount of "self-help" will make you the person God intended you to be. This transformation requires the Holy Spirit working in us, guiding us, convicting us, transforming us. I learned to "walk by faith, not by sight."[9] This doesn't mean that we close our eyes to what is around us, but that we trust the invisible power of the Holy Spirit over the visible difficulties.

Being transformed into a more Christ-like person means learning to see situations through a heavenly perspective. We surrender our ever-fearful, doubting, rebelling self-will, and we do not give in to self-condemnation. One of the greatest lessons I learned from Much Afraid was to not only endure the surrender of my will to God, but to practice acceptance with joy.

Much Afraid taught me by example to battle and wrestle with doubt, bitterness, self-pity, and resentment, to embrace sorrow and suffering, to overcome obstacles by faith. She also showed me how to rely on The Shepherd's guidance and courage. The Shepherd spoke to me as well as Much Afraid when he said, "This is the word I now leave with you. Believe it and practice it with joy. My sheep hear my voice and they follow me. Whenever you are willing to obey me, Much Afraid, and to follow the path of my choice, you will always be able to hear and recognize my voice, and when you hear it you must always obey. Remember also that it is always safe to obey my voice, even if it seems to call you to paths which look impossible or even crazy."[10]

The words "even crazy" stuck out to me. To the world, it is crazy to start with suffering and end with hope. But through faith in Christ by the power of his Holy Spirit, not only do we gain hope, but we also bring glory to God. Yes, Jesus promised we would have trouble in this world, but he followed that statement with a promise: "But take heart, for I have overcome this world."[11]

So now, let's take another look at Romans 5. This time, consider the verses surrounding verse 5:

"Therefore, since we have been justified through faith,
we have peace with God through our Lord Jesus Christ,
through whom we have gained access by faith into this
grace in which we now stand. And we boast in the hope
of the glory of God. Not only so, but we also glory in
our sufferings, because we know that suffering produces
perseverance; perseverance, character; and character,
hope. And hope does not put us to shame, because God's
love has been poured out into our hearts through the Holy
Spirit, who has been given to us."[12]

Isn't that amazing? We have been given grace and peace with God because of our faith in our Lord Jesus Christ. Our sufferings, perseverance and character bring us hope because God's love is in our hearts—and only because the Holy Spirit put it there! We can trust in The Shepherd and take him at his word, knowing that his promises are true. This is my hope: that my faith in The Shepherd will not fail me, but will transform me and fill my heart with his love.

The Shepherd's promises to Much Afraid were fulfilled when she arrived at The High Places and received her new name, Grace and Glory. Her companions, Sorrow and Suffering, also received new names: Joy and Peace. Just think, Much Afraid was traveling with Joy and Peace from the beginning! She just didn't recognize them as they truly were; she first needed to be transformed by The Shepherd and be given the eyes to see them.

HOPE, THE ANCHOR OF OUR SOULS

I don't know where you are on your journey, but I hope that when look back on your life, you can recognize areas in which you have been transformed, strengthened and changed along the way. But even more importantly, I pray that you keep your head up, your eyes on Jesus and your mind on the hope we have in Christ. This hope is alive and active! It comes from the Holy Spirit, who lives in us and intercedes for us before God. Hope is the anchor of our soul because we know we have been justified freely and have gained access to stand freely before God in grace—he calls us by a new name.[13] This hope will surely not disappoint.[14]

If hope is difficult for you to find right now, hear me say this: You are not alone. I know it hurts, but don't give up the search. Unfortunately, moving from glory to glory isn't always as delightful as it sounds when we're actually in the process of it. Sometimes, seasons of loss, loneliness and heartbreak have the greatest potential to make us more like Christ, because in those seasons, we actively seek him out and rely on him. But other times, we just feel so weary. *The wait has been so long. Things aren't getting better. Is God even listening to my prayers anymore?* Hope may seem elusive, or even non-existent. But we have this beautiful truth: When we are in Christ, hope is *always* available to us because it *lives in us.* We need only to be willing to trust in the hope of Christ to see the its fruit in our lives. Like the definition of faith found in Hebrews, "Faith is the reality of what is hoped for, the proof of what is not seen."[15]

Like Much Afraid experienced, hope comes when we choose to trust that God knows what is best for us. He is faithful and trustworthy, and he will bring us to the High Places with him. And by the time we get there, we'll be stronger, steadier and more like Christ because of the trials we faced along the way. When trust feels too hard, ask God to increase your faith. This prayer is totally in line with God's heart, and he loves answering it! Even when it feels like your path is winding out of control, or you're taking a detour in the wrong direction, know that when you are in Christ, your journey will always lead you back to him. The ups and downs will smooth out, and when you look back on where you started, you'll find evidence that you truly have grown in grace, from glory to glory.

Reflection Questions

1. What are some ways that knowing your story could influence your future?

2. How well do you to listen to God? How do you think reflecting on your life could change the way you listen to and rely on God?

3. Have you ever experienced the transformation of suffering turning into hope? How do you relate to Much Afraid's journey of finding strength and love as she walked with The Shepherd?

4. In what ways are you seeking hope right now? How might reflecting on your journey help you to recognize God's presence and provision along the way?

CHAPTER SEVEN

Making Sense of Your Story

Sharing your story with other people may be new for you. But I guarantee that *thinking* about your life as a story isn't. Historians, researchers and artists alike would agree that forming stories is a universal practice of the human experience. We have been using narratives to make sense of life and the world around us since the beginning of time. We grapple with meaning and seek to explain the inexplicable through story. Some have linked our inclination to form and share stories with survival instincts, while others believe it reflects our desire to solve existential problems.[1] Everyone agrees, though, that stories are an important aspect of humanity. We *want* them and we *need* them. We form stories to find resolution in our questions about life, purpose and eternity.

While thinking in terms of story may come naturally, we do not necessarily tell those stories accurately. Our stories are largely influenced by our perceptions and our worldview. The same story could be shared in multiple ways, and while each version may be *technically* true, the implications of one version might be much different from another. Thus, it is important to be mindful of how we internalize and share our own stories.

Unless we make a conscious effort to look beyond our narrow, personal experience, our story can be easily distorted. You might see yourself as the hero of all your stories. Through the lens of your story, you do everything right, and anything that goes wrong is someone else's fault. Or you might see yourself as a perpetual victim in your personal narrative, which would make it hard to believe your circumstances could ever improve. To find our place in the truest story, we need to take a step back and consider a larger perspective.

In a typical story, there is an initiating event. Something *good* goes terribly *wrong*. The ensuing story, then, describes how the protagonist strives to make right what has been broken. But there would be no story if there wasn't any conflict or tension along the way, right? The tension in stories comes from the antagonist—a person or set of circumstances that opposes the protagonist. Usually, when we tell stories, we tell ones that have already reached some sort of resolution. For example, you may tell about the day when you finally found a job after a season of unemployment. Or when you officially decided to date your new boyfriend/girlfriend after years of convincing yourself that you were "just friends."

Sometimes, even stories that have become ingrained in us—the events we could describe backwards and forwards—can be hard to articulate when we try sharing them with someone else. It becomes even *more* complicated when we try to share experiences that have not yet been resolved. Those things you are questioning and working through right now? They aren't only *becoming* part of your story—they *are* your story. Even when you are still struggling to make sense of a situation, you have a perspective that's worth sharing. You don't need to make it to "the other side" before your story has potential to encourage or inspire others. You hold wisdom within you. All you need to do is identify it.

In order to identify the wisdom of your story, it can be helpful to use a framework to process your experiences and thoughts. In this chapter, I'll share the framework I have found most helpful when reflecting on my story. This framework has challenged me to broaden my perspective and not look only at my current circumstances, but also look for opportunities to grow in that season. I encourage you to consider a situation in your own life that still needs resolution. Keep that situation in mind as we walk through the questions of "Why?" and "How?" to develop your story. My prayer is that you will step away from this chapter with clearer perspective and insight, and that you will be reassured of purpose and opportunity, even in the most difficult of seasons.

WHY IS FORMING A STORY IMPORTANT?

As I mentioned earlier, stories seem to be a natural part of the human experience. We tend towards story; it is our preferred method for making sense of the world. Story also has significant psychological benefits to it. James W. Pennebaker is a social psychologist who studies the relationships between language, health and social behavior. Many of his studies focus on storytelling and its associated health benefits, which include resolving emotional distress and healing from traumatic experiences.[2] An equally encouraging finding of these studies is that the healing power of forming a story has proven to be universal. Pennebaker writes,

Positive health and behavioral effects [from writing and forming a story about one's traumatic experiences] have been found with maximum-security prisoners, medical students, community-based samples of distressed crime victims, arthritis and chronic pain sufferers, men laid off from their jobs, and women who have recently given birth to their first child. These effects have been found in all social classes and major racial/ethnic groups in the United States, and in samples in Mexico City, New Zealand, French-speaking Belgium, and the Netherlands.[3]

Pennebaker explains that forming a story allows us to simplify our experiences. As we simplify our experiences over time, we are better able to manage them and find resolution. He says, "Once an experience has structure and meaning, it would follow that the emotional effects of that experience are more manageable. Constructing stories facilitates a sense of resolution, which results in less rumination and eventually allows disturbing experiences to subside gradually from conscious thought."[4]

But simplified stories don't need to be *simple* stories. And they certainly don't need to be easy or fabricated ones. Rather, simplified stories are forged in the work of processing them well. A story is manageable after dealing with it in a healthy way. The painful details may not disappear from our memory, but they can fade from our story when we find healing and resolution. We can own the full story, but be selective about which aspects we let define us. Brené Brown, a social psychologist and one of my favorite authors, explains this concept well:

The opposite of recognizing that we're feeling something is denying our emotions. The opposite of being curious is disengaging. When we deny our stories and disengage from tough emotions, they don't go away; instead, they own us, they define us. Our job is not to deny the story, but to defy the ending—to rise strong, recognize our story, and rumble with the truth until we get to a place where we think, Yes. This is what happened. This is my truth. And I will choose how this story ends.[5]

HOW DO I START FORMING MY STORY?

I have broken my reflection framework into four different elements of story: *Setting, Character, Plot* and *Theme.* Deconstructing your circumstances into each of these four components will give you the building blocks to form a cohesive story. To further explain each element of the reflection framework, I have interwoven threads of my own story. In the next chapter, you will see how these threads weave together to create a meaningful story that I can now share easily with others.

Let me give you context for the story I use in my examples, based on the four years I spent in college. During those four years, I attended just as many schools. Yup. That's right. I went to four different colleges in four years. It was unconventional and unplanned, and for the longest time, I was uneasy sharing this part of my story. I felt uncomfortable talking about because I felt like a failure. I would think, I *can't make up my mind. I can't stick to my decisions.* I feared what people thought of me. I wondered if they would see me as a flaky or uncommitted. And I worried that my zigzagging path through college would indicate that I had no idea how to listen to God or obey him. These fears distressed me. I felt insecure, defensive and doubtful I even *had* a story.

Now that the tension of my story is clear, let's dive into the reflection framework and start working towards a resolution.

SETTING

Setting is the place where your story happens. Setting can be a physical location: your house, a city, the university, your workplace, etc. But Setting can also be more nuanced: your setting may be affected by the cultural or political climate, the people you live with or see regularly, your family dynamics or the schedule you keep. Sometimes, the setting of our stories might span a wide timeframe. Childhood circumstances may have just as much effect on your story as circumstances in the present-day. Setting is important because your surroundings influence and shape you. The bottom line is this: Setting is a big element to your story. There are many different ways to consider which aspects of Setting have influenced your story. But don't let that overwhelm you; just take it one step at a time.

To live the life to which God has called us, it's important that we take an honest look at our lives and the circumstances that have shaped us. When we acknowledge the influences in our lives, both good and bad, we can choose to rise above the circumstances that weigh us down. We can form a personal story of who we are, where we've come from and where we're going. That story will help us to prioritize, make decisions, and be more attentive to the call of God on our lives.

To reflect on your setting, we'll start by creating what I call a "mind-map." Grab a notebook or a spare sheet of paper, or flip to page 105 of this book to find some extra space to write your notes in. In the middle of the page, write down a phrase that represents your conflict, the situation for which you seek resolution. Then fill the rest of the page with any thoughts or associated ideas that come to mind. You can start with the basics of Setting, such as location, time-frame and physical surroundings. Once you have those down,

I encourage you to dig in a little deeper. Here are some questions to guide you:

- What emotions do you feel about this situation? Why do you feel this way?

- What people come to mind when you think about this situation? How do they influence you?

- Have you ever experienced a situation like this in the past? If so, when? What happened?

- When did you become aware of this conflict? What caused you to recognize it?

- How is this situation affecting your life?

You can write your responses in whatever way fits you best. They can be messy scribbles, doodles, or single words neatly organized in rows. There is no right way to reflect; it's just important that you do. Below is a sample of my reflections on the setting that affected the transitions of my college years. As a reminder, this is only an example. Your reflections may be completely different in content or style, and that is totally okay.

- I had supportive parents who encouraged me to do my best and gave me freedom to make my own decisions. They expected me to graduate from college, but they allowed me to take my own path.

- I often heard the message that God has a plan and purpose for my life. I wanted to live in this plan and purpose, so I constantly sought to understand what God was calling me to do.

- I grew up in Grand Rapids, Michigan. Grand Rapids is a relatively conservative city with heavy Christian influence. When I moved to Tennessee, I was surprised by how different Christian culture looked in other regions of the United States.

- Each college I attended had its own culture and norms. I started to understand how much we are shaped by our surroundings.

- Most of my friends remained at the original schools they had chosen. This made me question myself and compare my decisions with theirs.

- My surroundings changed frequently as I transferred from college to college: different schools, different houses, different roommates. These changes allowed me to learn from a wide variety of people and experiences.

Viewing our physical location, circumstances and influences as Setting helps us take a step back. It gives us the space to see the pressures and expectations that surround us, without assuming that they define us. Take another look at your mind-map. What oppositions and or expectations do you face? Are there people or commitments that make it difficult for you to trust God? How might you be allowing your circumstances to define you rather than your identity as a forgiven, dearly-loved child of God?

God is the all-knowing God who holds you in the palm of his hand. He knows your every need even before you do. He sees the circumstances you face and knows the doubts you feel. God sees you. And he loves you.

We get a beautiful picture of God's intricate knowledge and care for us in Psalm 139:

"Lord, you have searched me and known me. You know when I sit down and when I stand up; you understand my thoughts from far away. You observe my travels and my rest; you are aware of all my ways. Before a word is on my tongue, you know about it, Lord. You have encircled me; you have placed your hand on me. This extraordinary knowledge is beyond me. It is lofty; I am unable to reach it."[6]

Let that truth sink is as we move on to reflecting on *Character*.

CHARACTER

When novelists prepare to write a story, one of the most important steps they take is completing a character study. A character study is essentially an in-depth analysis of the new fictional character who will lead the story. Different authors write character studies in different ways. Some writers will make a list of probing questions, then answer them from the character's point of view. Others may write out a possible letter from the character to a friend or lover. Still others will transcribe an imagined conversation between the character and his or her therapist. The point is, it doesn't matter so much *how* the author writes the character study, but that they do it. It would be awfully hard for the author to write a compelling novel if she didn't know her character very well, right?

Usually, when asked to describe ourselves, we share external facts, such as where we live, what we do and with whom we share our lives. While this is important information, it actually describes our setting more than our character. Analyzing ourselves as a character brushes away all of the external expectations that we feel define us. When we remove those surrounding expectations, we start to understand the unique and complex characteristics that make us who we are.

When we think of ourselves as characters, we are free to describe ourselves beyond our setting. A character study looks within a person, not around him or her. It is incredibly helpful to have a solid grasp on our identity so that we can understand our stories and how God moves in our lives. It is a practice of reflecting on who God created us to be, and boldly standing in that reality.

Character exploration is an exercise in identity and self-perception. It's where the rubber meets the road as we come face to face with who we are. Since we've already sifted out our circumstances and influences by describing our setting, we don't have anything to hide behind. Our situation is no longer a valid excuse for our behavior, our self-perception or our thoughts and actions towards other people. As we think of ourselves as characters in a story, we acknowledge our characteristics that are beautiful and our characteristics that we try to hide. It's time to get real with our pain, our fears, our judgments and our doubts—as well as our passions, our skills, our joys and our most treasured loves. We get to decide what we let define us. Will we allow ourselves to be defined by God, his grace and his purpose? This is a question answered through exploration of Character.

If you created your Setting mind-map on a different sheet of paper and still have room, add your character reflections to that page, or start a new one. You can find an additional page for Character reflection on page 106. What consistent characteristics do you notice in yourself? What skills or gifts do you believe God has equipped you with? What are you capable of achieving, solving or changing in the world? Here are some additional questions to aid your reflection:

- What challenges have you overcome that make you most proud? How were you able to do it?

- What embarrasses you most about yourself? Why does it embarrass you?

- What things do people tend to ask you for help with? How does this make you feel?

- What ideas or topics do you catch yourself daydreaming about?

- How do you react when you feel let-down or hurt? How do you respond when you feel loved or valued?

My prayer is that through this exercise, you would recognize that you are a handcrafted work of the Lord. He made you to be you, and no one else. God, who loves you so much, is the gift-giver of your interests, abilities, dreams, strengths and even your weaknesses. He is committed to using your life for a purpose greater than you can imagine.

My Character reflection during the time I spent in college is incredibly long and deeply personal. Nonetheless, I'll share a brief introduction to better illustrate the idea:

- I can be stubborn and like to get things right the first time.

- I have a variety of interests and talents I am interested in pursuing. Sometimes I'm afraid that I'll be "spread too thin" to really achieve success with any of them.

- I am sensitive to what the people around me think and how comfortable they feel.

- I have a deep reserve of passion. I am easily fired up, and I don't sit still for long when I know that I could help fill a need.

- I have a trusting heart. I tend to believe the best about people and circumstances. I have been wounded by this, but I intentionally work to keep my heart soft.

As we carry on through life, we change, grow and gain new perspective on engaging the world. With each new lesson learned, we better understand our character. We learn to make sense of our reactions, decisions and feelings that we couldn't quite explain in the moment. It can be discouraging when our stories don't seem to add up or when there are unanswered questions. You may be tempted to give up the effort of reflecting on your story. But please, keep at it. Take note of your thoughts, feelings and responses. Reflect on them. Make connections between them. Doing so practices conscious living, and it will have significant impact on the direction of your story's *Plot*.

PLOT

The plot of a story is the series of events that affect a character and ultimately transform him or her. Plot-points in our own stories tend to be major events—significant changes in our life or decisions that shaped us. Plot helps us to identify the major moments in our lives that have defined us. We can then chart them out and find connections between them. This helps us recognize our purpose, intention and meaning in life as we analyze the plot and trajectory of our path. It can guide us to make decisions that maintain our trajectory, or possibly alter it if we don't like where we're headed.

I find Plot such an exciting thing to reflect on. Often, I am unable to find peace in my current circumstances until I stop to consider what is actually taking place and how it might tie into the larger picture. I find myself constantly amazed by the intricate ways that God chooses to work his will. Reflecting on Plot reminds me that God's ways are the best ways. Even when I feel like he isn't doing anything or that he's forgotten me, I look at the plot of my story and I am reminded that God is always on the move, working everything out for his glory and my good.

Along with helping us identify overarching themes in our lives, Plot helps us deal with the more intricate or painful experiences of life. When we resolve these areas with story, we can find healing and confidence to share with others. As we reflect on Plot, you will likely think of your painful seasons, as well as many wonderful, proud moments. They all fold into each other, the way waves do as they approach the shore, making one cohesive story. Plot helps me to understand that each season was necessary to bring me to where I am now, growing in my maturity and deepening in my knowledge of God. Below is a list of reflection questions to help you consider your own story's plot. Walk through the following questions on your mind-map. You can find space to reflect on Plot on page 107.

- What are the biggest or bravest decisions you've ever made? What influenced those decisions? How did those decisions impact your life?

- What events have most notably "interrupted" or altered your life's course? How? What changed as a result of those events?

- What fears or doubts repeatedly hold you back from pursuing new opportunities? Where do you think these fears originate?

- When have you felt closest to God? What was going on at that time? What specifically made you feel close to God?

- When have you felt furthest from God? What was going on at that time? What specifically made you feel far from God?

For additional ideas as you get started, I have shared a few examples of my own Plot reflections below. Keep in mind that this is only a small sample of my life's plot-points:

- I am proud of my decision to spend the summer after my junior year of high school in Ecuador, where I learned from and served with a missionary organization.

- Being invited to lead and serve on mission trips through my church and youth group definitely changed the course of my life. Before taking these opportunities, my concerns had been mostly focused on popularity in school and boys.

- I'm afraid of being average. I worry about making mistakes that might ruin my credibility. I want to lead and help others well, but I am so aware of my own inadequacies that I often doubt my ability.

- I have felt closest to God while serving on mission trips or at Christian camps. I think this is because I was more aware of my need for God and I sensed his realness. I spent more time in prayer and listening to him.

- I have felt furthest from God when I have been overwhelmed—when my problems have felt too big and immediate. Sometimes, it has been when I feel pressured to make a big decision; other times, it has been when a friend of mine was really hurting and I didn't know what to do. I have usually tried to solve these problems on my own, instead of going to God first.

As I reflect on the plot elements that influenced my college decisions, I keep coming back to one major theme: God was pursuing my heart and stirring within me a desire to follow him wherever he might lead—no matter the cost. We'll cover *Theme* next, but for now, consider which of your own plot-points stand out the most. Which ones demonstrate the greatest evidence of God working in and through you? The most important thing to remember about Plot is that, ultimately, we are not the ones in control. "A man's heart plans his way, but the Lord determines his steps."[7]

THEME

Are you ready to start piecing together all of your different reflections into a story? That is what Theme is all about. It involves analyzing each of the different elements of your story—your Setting, Character and Plot—and finding the purpose in them all. This is where you'll start making realizations like, "Hey, I grew a lot because of situation A, which enabled me to make a better decision in situation B, and that explains why I'm now in situation C." Or, "Over and over again, God has been leading me into this same type of situation in which I've really needed to rely on him." Or, "I keep coming back to a certain issue or cause. I wonder if God may be calling me to invest in it more?"

I don't have a set of reflection questions for you to work through regarding Theme. Instead, your task is to go back to your previous reflections and look for common threads. What ideas or situations keep reappearing? How has your setting influenced your character? How has your setting affected your life's plot? How has your plot changed your character? The list could go on and on. There is space to write out your reflections on page 108.

Writing your reflections down is helpful so that you can visualize the different elements. Are there any outliers that don't seem to fit in with the rest? Does your reflection seem to build towards one major theme, or several smaller ones? How might the themes you've identified connect with your understanding of God's character? How do they affect the way you see yourself? What about the way you perceive your future? You don't need to know exactly where you're going, but in what direction are you headed? What do you feel the Lord calling you to? What does obedience look like in this season of life?

These are all questions to ponder over time. You may not be able to spot a theme immediately, especially if any unresolved circumstances are ongoing. Pray for God's wisdom and guidance as you look for meaning and a storyline in your experiences. We have hope that we are not the ones writing our stories, nor are we tasked with finding or creating purpose for our lives. That's God's job; our job is to trust him and press in where he leads us. May our prayers echo those of King David's: "I call to God Most High, to God who fulfills his purpose for me."[8] God's purposes are much sweeter and richer than any we could imagine. The years I spent bouncing around from college to college, chasing purpose and meaning, taught me this lesson well. I'm excited to share more of this journey with you in the next chapter. But for now, enjoy the goodness that comes from reflecting on *your* journey.

SETTING

Use this page for your reflections on setting.

CHARACTER

Use these pages for your reflections on character.

PLOT

Use these pages for your reflections on plot.

THEME

Use these pages for your reflections on theme.

CHAPTER EIGHT

Own Your Story and Give God the Glory

The summer after high school graduation, I packed my bags and, along with my family, I road-tripped down to Jackson, Tennessee. I received many questions about why I chose to attend Union University, and I didn't have any clear answers. "I just like it, and I want to go there," was my best response. My parents, gracious and supporting beyond words, said, "Okay," and left the rest of their questions unanswered. After helping to set up my new dorm room, my family returned to Michigan, while I stayed in that tiny town amidst the flat, cotton fields of western Tennessee. Attending Union University didn't make much sense to the people around me, but I felt confident about my decision. I was excited to chart my own adventure, and I envisioned myself putting down roots in Tennessee post-graduation. But that's not how things turned out; I only spent one semester at Union. And as you know from earlier chapters, it was certainly a challenging semester for me. But hear me when I say this: the hard parts of that season don't negate the beauty and growth that were also present. *The same is true in your story.*

Moving to Tennessee caused me unexpected, hard-core culture shock. Southern belles are a real thing, and I quickly recognized that I wasn't one. The friends I made at Union were sweet, generous and some of the most beautiful women I know—inside and out. These women were also so in touch with their feminine side, that I almost felt like I didn't have one. In contrast with my new friends, I was loud, opinionated and independent. My directness felt coarse compared to their polished politeness. Some friends excused my personality differences by saying, "She's a Northerner." I didn't quite understand the stereotype, but I reluctantly accepted it. Now, I don't actually believe that the differences I experienced can be fully explained by the Northern-Southern divide, nor am I suggesting that either personality style is better or more desirable than the other. But the reality is that there was a stark difference between me and my new friends. I began to question womanhood and the qualities that set women apart from men.

In fact, I began questioning everything. I recognized racial tension and the stark reality of white privilege in Jackson that I hadn't noticed before. I heard more arguments over church denominations than I ever cared to hear, which challenged me to dig into my own theology. I wondered why so many of my new girlfriends aspired to be pastor's wives, but didn't seem to consider how they had been gifted to serve in their own ministries. And I was concerned that staying in Tennessee might prevent me from having close relationships with my family in the future. I was all over the place—which became the theme of the next four years of my life. It may seem silly to say, but sometimes I wonder if I was meant to be at Union so that I could learn how to ask questions and pursue their answers.

After my first semester at Union, I attended an accelerated winter course called, "Training to Walk Daily with Jesus"—how cool is that? The discipleship class was taught by an incredibly wise professor, who proved to be transformational in my walk with Christ. We spent the final week of the class at a monastery for a silent retreat. My prayer that week was, *God, I want to trust you more. Help me to love you with my whole heart. Teach me to follow you step by step.* God spoke clearly to me during my stay at the monastery. He gave me a vision of moving back to Grand Rapids and living in a house with other young women. Not only that, but I felt him telling me that the house was to welcome teen moms.

I was excited and overwhelmed. I didn't know how to figure out the next step, or even if this vision was actually from God or just my imagination. But deep in my heart, I felt peace, and that peace allowed me to trust that it was from God. So I prayed, *God, if this is really from you, I need you to confirm it. Prepare my parents for this news, and help them to see that this is your idea. I can't do this alone, Lord. Give me a friend to do this with me.*

Sure enough, God confirmed the vision he'd given me. He answered my prayers—but in *his* timing and in *his* ways, not my own. My parents, who I thought would be disappointed by me dropping out of college, listened to everything I told them. Then they responded with the most life-giving words: "We see that God is working in you, and we support you." God also put a friend on my heart. I heard him telling me that my friend Amanda would be the one to join me in this mission. So I called her up and shared my vision. She was hesitant at first. To be fair, I'm sure I pitched the idea to her in a far too intense way, saying something like, "I just *know* that God is calling us to do this!" Amanda ended up telling me "no" a couple of days after I had withdrawn from Union. I had just moved all my belongings back into my parents' house, and my heart dropped when she gave me her answer. I was devastated and confused. I remember running for miles on the treadmill in my parents' basement that night, trying to rid myself of the anxious knot in my chest. I started to doubt what the Lord had showed me. Had I made it all up in my head? Did God trick me, only to hang me out to dry? I feared that I had arrived at the end of my story. I thought, *Is this who I am now? A college drop-out with an embarrassingly shattered big dream?*

Thankfully, that season of uncertainty was short. Only two weeks after I had moved home, Amanda called. She said, "Jen, you're never going to believe this." Then she told me a story that just about knocked the wind out of me. Amanda had just been asked to move into a house with another friend and her newborn baby. You see where this is going, don't you? Yep. I was invited to live in that house, too. And not long after, we all moved in. Three friends and a precious baby, all together in a house in Grand Rapids— just as God had shown me. I was rocked by God's faithfulness and provision. He is so clever in the ways he makes good on his promises, isn't he?

After having the spring semester and summer off from school, I was ready to go back to school in the fall. I chose to attend Cornerstone University, a small Christian college in Grand Rapids. Looking back on the year I spent at Cornerstone, I don't remember too much about the college itself—only the wonderful people I met, the weekly Wednesday morning chapels and the Sunday evening worship services. That year of my life was marked by feelings of severe loneliness. I had friends, but not many who really *knew* me. It was apparent to me that my many moves had hindered deep relationships from blossoming. When I would check social media, I'd see that my friends who had stayed at their colleges had tight-knit friend groups. I, on the other hand, had a random network of friends all over the place. I felt alone, and I didn't know how to thank God in the midst of my loneliness.

While this season of loneliness was bitter, it drove me to rely on God. I didn't have many social outlets, so I spent a lot of time reading my Bible. I fell in love with it. For the first time in my life, I started to rely on God's Word like daily bread.[1] I would go for walks around a nearby lake and pray the whole time. I would go to coffee shops to read and journal. Of course, there were good days and bad days. My good days were the days when I stayed calm and confident of God's love for me. My bad days were the days when I viewed my lack of friends as a lack of God's care for me. I would push God away in anger, instead of embracing his deep, wide and incomprehensible love for me.[2]

That winter, a family from my church asked me to house-sit for a month while they traveled. To me, that month felt like the epitome of loneliness—just me and a dog, alone in a house in the stillness of winter. I cried a lot in that house, begging God for deeper friendships. One night, in the middle of my tears, my phone rang. My friends Alyssa and Jehricole were nearby the house, and asked if they could stop by. "YES! Of course," I responded. They arrived at the house within minutes, and we stayed up so late chatting that they decided to spend the night. I had a hard time falling asleep that night because I was so happy. And shortly after that spontaneous sleepover, I noticed God answering my prayers for deeper friendships. Soon enough, I was amazed by the women God had blessed me with: Alyssa, Jehricole, Jilly, Kate, Julie, Abby, Kelsey, Maddie, and three different girls named Amanda (no joke). These women became my community. I had the gift of sharing life with them and learning from them. I finally got a taste for what "community" meant, and it was especially sweet after experiencing the pain of loneliness.

After my sophomore year of college, I decided to switch to a local state school, Grand Valley State University (GVSU). My goal was to graduate within four years, and I needed a bigger school that offered more classes in order to accomplish that goal. I started at GVSU with pretty low expectations. My schedule was already full with a part-time job, volunteering and time with friends. I approached school with a "get in, get out" mentality—I took as many courses at once as I could, and I didn't spend much time socializing or building connections on campus (with the exception of a guy named Trevor, who would later become my husband.) We met the first week of classes, and I was *definitely* intentional about building that relationship!).

Even though I wasn't the most engaged student on campus by any means, I learned a lot from my time at GVSU. I discovered that I appreciated conversations that challenged my thoughts and beliefs. I enjoyed sharing classes with diverse groups of students. I started searching out opportunities to discuss big issues with people who held different worldviews. These discussions spurred me to think deeper and more creatively about my own experiences and the roots of my deeply-held beliefs. Finally, two years later, I walked across the graduation stage in my shiny, royal-blue robe. I was proud, yes, but what I felt even more than pride was gratitude for God's grace upon me.

TO GOD BE THE GLORY

The four years I spent in college were crazy. Not only did I frequently switch schools, but I also frequently switched my major. At different points along the way, I had declared a linguistics major, a teaching major and a Spanish major, but in the end, I graduated with a writing degree.

While my zigzagging path through college is humorous to me now, having come out on the other side, I tried to hide that part of my story while I was in the midst of it. I felt ashamed, and feared what others would think of my choices. I wondered if all the changes and moves I had made reflected a major character flaw. My story seemed to scream, "flaky," "uncommitted," "indecisive" and "failure." I worried that I would be perceived as inconsistent and that people would doubt my trustworthiness because I didn't stick to my original decisions.

By the time my senior year came to a close, I had gained enough perspective to realize it was best to accept my story as it was. Of course, I had made mistakes and bad decisions along the way. I *had* been flaky at times, and I *had* occasionally let myself and others down. But that wasn't the totality of my story. My college experience wasn't just the story of a confused girl, unsure of which passions to pursue. It was a reflection of a much bigger story: the story of a loving God who knew all my inner workings, dreams and gifts, and his plan to use those things for his glory. And in the process, he was making me more like him, too.

Each new university had its own sub-culture that challenged me to see people, and myself, in a new way. Each transition came with some pain, but also the gift of growth. The constant changes broadened my ideas of God's will, intentionality and community.

I gained plenty of opportunities to practice trusting God and stepping out in faith to follow him. And while I may have changed my major often, God has been faithful to bear fruit through each skill. I have used my linguistics and Spanish knowledge to translate and communicate with new friends during mission trips to Mexico. My brief exposure to teaching methods has helped me in youth ministry to teach God's Word more effectively. Finally, my writing education has helped me communicate what Lord puts on my heart in order to encourage others.

IT'S NOT ABOUT US AFTER ALL

I imagine that your story has some similarities to the one I just shared. Maybe you're wrestling with similar questions, doubts or transitions. While God's faithfulness during my college years is special to me, I know it is not novel. It seems as if most people are in a constant state of change. Our lives are made up of puzzle pieces that sometimes seem polarized, but somehow fit together. As Christians, I think we find this to be true even more often. When we trust God with our lives and follow his leading, all of our ventures and experiences add together to make a sum greater than its parts.

This is because it's not about us after all. If the purpose of our lives was to make a name for ourselves—to become great, memorable and successful—then maybe life wouldn't be full of so many surprises. We'd chart out a road-map to success, and we'd stick to it at all costs. We would make choices that aligned with our plans, not the plans of an Almighty God.

As followers of Christ, however, we must willingly give up our independence. We must acknowledge the reality that we can't do this on our own, and that we are in need of a Savior. The life of a Christian is one that gives up the right to pursue selfish desires, and instead lives sold-out to God's glory. We must be conscious of the cost and make the choice to willingly follow Christ. Unfortunately, many of us get distracted along the way. The walk of faith does not necessarily provide security, and it can be tempting to seek that security over God's will in our lives. But when we choose obedience to God, we get to partake in the stories of God's greatness, love and grace. And then we get the joy of sharing it with others.

When we surrender our plans, goals and treasures to God, he takes them and multiplies them into a story far greater than we could have ever dreamed ourselves. If you feel like your skills or talents seem insignificant compared to the calling that the Lord has put on your heart, I dare you to ask him to use you anyway. God loves a willing heart, and he loves to blow our minds by taking something small and using it in extraordinary ways.

Remember the Bible story of the fish and loaves of bread? In Matthew 14, we read a story of Jesus teaching a large group of people. And when I say large, I mean five-thousand-people large. As Jesus was speaking to and healing these people, they were so engrossed in his message that no one left to take a break or find food. They were far from the nearest town, and the disciples realized that if the people didn't leave soon, they'd be stuck in the countryside without food.

The disciples talked to Jesus and suggested that he dismiss the group to go find some food. Much to their surprise, Jesus responded, "You give them something to eat."[3] All the disciples had with them were five loaves of bread and two fish, and they didn't see how that was going to help the five thousand people in the crowd. Jesus asked the disciples to bring him the fish and bread. When they did, he blessed it, divided it up and handed it to the disciples. Jesus instructed the disciples to distribute the food to the crowd. To everyone's amazement, the food multiplied as it was passed out. The five loaves of bread and two fish appeared so insignificant from the disciples' perspective, but when this food was given over to Jesus in faith, it fully satisfied the hunger of five thousand people—and there were even twelve baskets of food left over!

Sometimes, it feels like when God calls us to something, we need to show up and make it happen. When God told the disciples to give the crowd something to eat, they looked around and panicked. How were they going to feed five thousand people? There was no way their five loaves and two fish would feed even a fraction of the people. Would they need to walk and find food for everyone all by themselves? I'm sure that there was a lot of worry, confusion and doubt in that moment.

It's important for us to keep in mind that when God calls us to something, he invites us into *his* work. It's not about us being able to perform, measure up or produce the right answer. When God calls us to something, he displays his glory and makes himself known in new ways. God will always equip us for the work he calls us to. And when he does, we get to be astonished by him and invite other people into that astonishment by sharing our story.

OUR STORIES DON'T CHANGE, BUT OUR PERSPECTIVE DOES

Do you see the difference perspective can make? When the disciples thought that *they* needed to feed the five thousand, the task was impossible. However, when their perspective changed and they saw that Jesus would do the feeding, the task was not only possible, but it was a story worth sharing *over and over again.* Every time that story is told, God is glorified.

The same thing happens with our stories, including my own. When I view my life as simply *my* story and a reflection of myself, it is empty, confusing and lacking purpose. However, when my perspective is corrected and honors God as the one in control of my life, the beauty and purpose in all of my life's twists and turns is evident. He uses all experiences for our good and for his glory. When we tell our stories to give God the credit, his glory is multiplied.

I'm not suggesting that you edit your stories to make them happy and "smiley" all the time. There can be a tendency in the church to sugar-coat difficult situations or offer trite, spiritual phrases instead of really engaging with each other's stories—pain and all. Sometimes, it can feel like incorporating God into our everyday conversations will come across as fake or cheesy. To be honest, sometimes it does. But that often happens when we are too worried about what the other person will think that we don't talk about God like he is a regular part of our lives. Allow others a glimpse into your personal relationship with God. Talk about him like he is your friend, your counselor, your protector and your king—because he *is*. You can show that your relationship with God is important to you without "pushing" your beliefs onto the other person. It's possible, and it's so much more attractive.

When your perspective is accurate, noticing the parallels between your life and God's greater story will become second-nature. The closer you hold that relationship, the easier it will be to walk in faith and confidence as God prepares and equips you along the way. Talking about God to people who don't care about him or don't believe in him might not be easy, but it will become much more natural as you recognize the role that God plays in your life on a daily basis.

FINDING PARALLELS BETWEEN OUR EXPERIENCES AND GOD'S STORY

So how do we figure out what God's story is? If God's story spans eternity, how do we find parallels between his story and our own lives? It may seem to be a daunting task.

The best person to teach us about God's story is God himself. He has blessed us with the Bible: his very own words that include an account of his character and his plan for the world. God gave us the Bible for us to know him and his will. Yes, that's right—the will of God is not hidden. Sometimes we get caught up in questions like, "Am I really doing God's will?" or, "Is this really what God wants for me?" We ask those questions almost hypothetically, as if there is no way to actually find the answer. But in fact, God has made his will clear to us throughout his word:

"He made known to us the mystery of his will, according
to His good pleasure that he planned in him for the
administration of the days of fulfillment—to bring
everything together in the Messiah, both things in heaven
and things on earth in him."
- Ephesians 1:4-10

God's will brings everything together in Jesus. That is God's ultimate plan, and that is his story. He will reconcile everything to himself through Christ. Other passages in the Bible teach us more about God's heart and the story he's writing. We learn about his desire for everyone to know him and be saved through Christ.[4] We learn that his story includes proclaiming good news to the poor, binding up the brokenhearted and freeing captives.[5]

If it seems overwhelming and confusing to reconcile your

story with God's story, ask God to open your eyes to his truth in the Scriptures and the difference those truths make in your life today. Ask God what he's doing and how you can be a part of it. You might not notice any instant changes, but I assure you: God will be delighted, and he will answer those prayers. In the next chapter, we'll discuss how to learn more about God's character and how it can affect our own identities.

Reflection Questions

1. What parts of your story do you need to take responsibility for? How could owning those parts of your story help you to find freedom?

2. How would you describe the perspective you have towards your story right now? Is it a perspective that makes you the center of your story, or God?

3. Imagine the ways that God could use your story to glorify him. How does this make you feel? Are you willing to let him use your story in that way?

4. What parallels do you see between your story and God's bigger story?

CHAPTER NINE

Root Your Identity

"Listen to Me, you who pursue righteousness, you who seek the Lord: Look to the rock from which you were cut, and to the quarry from which you were dug" - Isaiah 51:1

When we recognize God's character and presence in our lives, we are able to share our story from the perspective that God is in control, that he loves us, and that he desires the best for us. What we believe about God's character significantly impacts the way we live and what we believe about ourselves. It transforms our sense of self and helps us find our identity. If your experience has been like mine, you may have heard dozens of lessons on identity in church settings. Even so, please don't tune out on this one.

There's a reason we need to be reminded of God's character and our identity so frequently. Not only are we quick to forget who God is, but we also live in a culture that makes it very difficult to find contentment and satisfaction. We are fed an ever-increasing list of ideals and expectations through advertisements and media. Every day, we receive thousands of messages telling us what we need in order to fit in, find happiness or be loved. Instead of finding our identity in God, we are prone to identify ourselves by our jobs, family, appearance, wealth or marital status. While these various circumstances may *contribute* to our sense of self, we must be careful about letting them *define* our sense of self. The only appropriate place to root our identities is in God himself.

Rooting our identity in God should not be a burden. It's how we find freedom and life to the full. So whether you daily consider your identity in God or have never done so, join me for a refreshing jump into the cool waters of truth. May we be revitalized in our awe of God as we reflect on his nature and our role as his forgiven, dearly-loved children.

I encourage you to keep Isaiah 51:1 at the forefront of your mind. Whenever you question your identity, your purpose or your obedience in a particular season, "look to the rock from which you were cut." Look to God, for it is in God's image that we were created. God is love, and through his love, we learn how to love ourselves and others. The same is true for other attributes of God's character. He is justice, peace, mercy, forgiveness—the list goes on and on. If we want to grow in the fruits of the Spirit—love, joy, peace, patience, goodness, kindness, faithfulness and self-control—we need to look to God for direction. The more you know God, the more you will be able to see his guidance in your story. When you know this part of your story, you will be able to use it to spread the gospel as you share how God has healed you, comforted you and set you free. Your very life will be the evidence.

CHARACTERISTICS OF GOD

Some of my favorite Bible passages for learning more about God's character are found in the books of Genesis, Psalms and Isaiah. Genesis is an introduction to God. I find it fascinating how he introduces and reveals himself to humanity. We learn in Genesis that God is a God of order: he is a creator, a healer, a miracle-worker. He is faithful, just, forgiving and jealous for us. Here is a snapshot of names used for God throughout Genesis:

- Creator (Genesis 1:1)

- God Almighty (Genesis 17:1)

- Most High God (Genesis 15:2)

- The God who sees (Genesis 16:13)

- Judge of all the earth (Genesis 18:25)

- Eternal God (Genesis 21:33)

- The Lord, our Provider (Genesis 22:14)

- Shepherd (Genesis 49:15)

In the Psalms, we gain a deeper understanding of God's intimacy with his people. We are encouraged to look upon God's beauty and proclaim his glory. The Psalms also teach us to run to God when we are broken, afraid or angry. We are reminded of God's steadfast love in the midst of trials. A sample of the names used for God throughout the Psalms is included below:

- King (Psalm 10:16)

- Deliverer (Psalm 18:2)

- Shepherd (Psalm 23:1)

- Light (Psalm 27:1)

- The Lord our Peace (Psalm 29:11)

- Refuge & Strength (Psalm 62:7)

- Everlasting God (Psalm 90:2)

Isaiah is a powerful book in the Bible full of prophesies about Jesus. Reading Isaiah leaves me totally stunned, in awe of God's sovereignty and grace. We see Jesus as a servant, a warrior and the savior of the world. We are reminded in Isaiah that God fulfills every promise he speaks. Here are some of the ways the book of Isaiah describes God:

- Lord of Hosts (Isaiah 1:24)

- Holy One (Isaiah 43:15)

- The Lord who heals (Isaiah 53:5)

- Redeemer (Isaiah 54:8)

- Father (Isaiah 64:8)

When you read a passage of Scripture, ask yourself, "What does this say about God?" Then take it a step further and ask, "What are the implications of this truth for my life?" or "How have I seen this truth play out in my own life?" The books of Genesis, Psalms, and Isaiah are a couple of my favorite books in the Bible, but because "all Scripture is inspired by God and is profitable for teaching, for rebuking, for correcting, for training in righteousness,"[1] you can practice this reflection exercise in any Biblical passage.

For example, let's look at Psalm 19:7: "The instruction of the Lord is perfect, renewing one's life; the testimony of the Lord is trustworthy, making inexperienced wise."[2] From this verse, we learn several things about God. First, God is perfect, and out of his perfection, he created the laws of the earth. Second, because God's instruction is aligned with his perfection, it is for our own good to follow it. We can trust that following God's commandments will lead us closer to him and grow us in wisdom. The implication of this verse on my life is that no matter how tempting an opportunity may seem, it won't be worth it in the long-run if it goes against God and his commands. Therefore, even though I may not feel like it at the time, I should choose obedience, because it will honor God and benefit me. I have experienced this in my own life hundreds of times. I haven't always made the right choice, but regardless, I have recognized the truth that obedience to God is always the best option.

Our perceptions of God are influenced by so many factors, including our church experiences, our families, and our conversations with others. A.W. Tozer once said, "What comes to our minds when we think about God is the most important thing about us."[3] It's true. If we forget that God is in control and that he loves us with an incomprehensible, unconditional love, we will live differently than we do when we are aware of and rest in the promises of his unchanging character. When life throws a curveball and our stories feel uncertain, we can trust in God's sovereignty and good will towards us.[4] When we feel hurt or abandoned, we can rest in the knowledge that God is near to the brokenhearted.[5] When we feel afraid and helpless, we can call on our God who saves us.[6]

OUR IDENTITY

Just as we need to understand who God says he is, we need be rooted in the truth of who God says we are. The truths in Scripture about our identity are our arsenal for extinguishing the lies of insignificance, shame or failure. But these truths will also swiftly humble us when we struggle with pride, selfishness or envy. We draw conclusions about our potential and worth based on the thoughts we think about ourselves. If we aren't intentional about rooting these thoughts in truth, they can spiral downward quickly during a bad day or difficult season. That negative self-talk easily converts into over-generalizations about our self-worth. For example, we might tell ourselves, *I make everyone uncomfortable when I speak up in groups. I'm awkward. I should just keep my mouth shut.* Or maybe, *I'm really lonely. Everyone else seems to have lots of friends or a significant other, and I'm just alone. What's wrong with me? What if no one ever loves me? I'll be alone forever.*

The problem with these self-talk stories is that the feelings conveyed are valid, but the verdict is not. We take action and make decisions based on what we believe about ourselves. We need to make sure that we believe what is true, whole and necessary to living life fully. Take note of the stories you tell yourself. If you don't like what you find, ask God to help you see yourself from his perspective. Every negative thought or doubt we have about ourselves should be checked against the truth of the Bible. I hold these truths from Scripture especially close to my heart:

- I am a child of God. (John 1:12)

- I have been justified and redeemed. (Romans 3:24)

- I am an heir with Christ. (Romans 8:17)

- My body is God's temple because his Spirit lives in me. (1 Corinthians 6:17)

- I am a new creation in Christ. (2 Corinthians 5:17)

- I am complete in Christ. (Colossians 2:10)

- God supplies all my needs. (Philippians 4:19)

- God loves me and has chosen me. (1 Thessalonians 1:4)

- God's power works through me. (Ephesians 3:7)

- I am not alone. (Hebrews 13:5)

- God will perfect the work he has begun in me. (Philippians 1:6)

- I can forgive others. (Ephesians 4:32)

Aren't those truths spectacular? I can hardly believe them. God allows *me* to be a co-heir with Christ? God is willing to work through *me*? The Holy Spirit lives within *me*? It seems too amazing. Yet, the Spirit that is within me whispers, "It's true. This is how I see you." And it's that very Spirit that gives me faith to believe it. But even though I believe these things are true, I fail consistently to live up to them. I am angry, jealous, fearful and lazy on a daily basis. I need hourly conviction, grace and reminders that my God is who he says he is, and that I am who he says I am.

Several years ago, the Lord inspired a poem in my heart after reading Isaiah 26. It portrays the constant need for me to root my identity in him, and how easily I wander when I take my eyes off of him. Since then, I've copied the same poem in several of my journals, as I have needed the reminder over and over again. I thought it would be fitting to share with you. Maybe this poem of prayer echoes the cry of your own heart:

Bring Your Spirit

Bring your convicting Spirit on me;

Once again, humble me.

Bring me to a place of complete reliance on Thee.

All of the ugliness within me,

I'm asking you to expose.

I'm willing and waiting to be broken apart,

Trusting your promise that you will renew me.

You will build me up, uplifting me from the pit of despair,

Of denial, disgust, distrust,

And nights spent looking at myself in utter disbelief

That you would ever love someone as fallen as me.

And so here I am,

Falling, falling on my knees.

In humility, in adoration,

In complete awe of your holy name.

I understand why it was necessary that your Son came.

Every desire of mine, every fiber of my being

Has been drenched and tainted with sin.

I am in absolute need of a Savior,

The one who will justify my case in front of the only righteous King.

Oh, my Lord; oh, my Lord!

You have already paid my price in full!

Root Your Identity

I praise your name; I tingle with joy!

All of my emotion wells up to a cry

That you have called my name;

You have set me free!

By your beautiful, perfect blood

I have been completely and finally redeemed!

The city walls of lies, comfort and shame

That I had built so carefully around my heart

Were nothing strong enough to keep you out.

You have turned them into a pile of stones, completely destroyed.

And from that brokenness, a new temple is being built;

Created, refashioned, far more beautiful than before.

Because I am yours.

I give you my heart.

I bow my life at your will.

This softening of spirit came through tribulation.

One that showcased my defiance, pride and shame.

But you have turned it around to bless your holy name!

I long for you in the night;

Yes, the Spirit within me diligently seeks you.

For when your judgments are in the land,

The inhabitants of the world will learn righteousness.

And this is the promise I cling to;

That you will teach me righteousness.

You will continue to form my heart, will and life to yours.

So that I may be in tune with

Your perfect plan for redemption of your beautiful creation.

For you have lifted up my face and filled me with hope.

I will not hide this truth I have received.

Amen.

THE RELATIONSHIP BETWEEN IDENTITY AND CONFIDENCE

For most of my life, confidence has been a confusing concept for me. I don't think I'm alone in this, either. Personally, I've identified the root of my difficulty with confidence as the misconception that confidence and pride are basically the same. In my attempt to not be prideful, conceited or bossy, I've often also let go of my confidence, which left me insecure and striving.

Confidence is on-trend with today's culture. There are countless resources and campaigns on cultivating confident leadership, presenting with confidence and developing body confidence. Each of these forms of confidence is important in its own right. But what if, instead of addressing the symptoms of insecurity and low self-esteem, we dealt with the root problem? The root of these different issues is in our self-worth. And the best way to recognize our self-worth is by owning our identity as God's children. The God of all creation knows you by name. He loves you and lives in you. There is no disputing your worth when you acknowledge these truths. Trusting your identity as a forgiven, dearly-loved child of God will bring you the deepest confidence.

Confidence is not pride, nor selfishness, nor conceit when its roots are in Christ. Confidence is the peace within yourself that God has created you uniquely and uses you for his glory just as you are. Seek confidence in the unique gifts you have. Don't shy away from ambition, leadership or opportunities to use the gifts you've been given. Take seriously your value and the wisdom God has offered you. Share it with the world. When you act and speak out of a well of God-given confidence, your life will resonate with others.

VALUING YOUR STORY HELPS OTHERS VALUE THEIRS

Confidence gives way to authenticity. And authenticity creates connections that open up opportunities to find common ground. Therefore, don't be afraid to shine brightly in your confidence, because doing so will draw people to you. We know when someone is comfortable in their own skin; we sense each other's confidence and insecurity. When you are with a friend who is confident in herself and knows her worth, you feel free to be yourself, too. Let's resolve to be lights of encouragement to the people around us. We don't need to wait for permission to change the way we see ourselves, nor do we need to wait until we see others doing so. We can love ourselves now, just the way we are. When you find confidence in yourself and your story, you will notice a difference in how people open up to you. People are drawn to authenticity, so by displaying it in your life, you demonstrate one of the most compelling testimonies possible.

What insecurities tend to keep you from valuing your story? How do they present themselves? It's time to name them and put a stop to them. Take a pen and paper and write out the doubts and uncertainties that keep you from walking confidently. Where do they come from? Yourself? Your parents? Your boss? Your friends? What can you do to develop confidence in your areas of insecurity? We might not be able to rid ourselves of all our barriers to confidence right away, but we can take the first step. Our self-worth is closely tied to our openness and willingness to share our stories. Let's not waste time believing lies when we could be ministering to other souls and sharing the glory of God.

One of the most beautiful things about confidence is how it spreads from one person to another. It is a radiant attribute in a person; it shines brightly, and, at the same time, illuminates the beauty of surrounding people. Your confidence is a powerful tool in unlocking purpose and self-worth in others. When your confidence is rooted in God's love and grace, your light will have energy to spark many other wicks into flame. Your confidence will not hurt that of someone else; rather, it will encourage and inspire others to live more fully in their God-given identity. Confidence, when met with confidence, only burns brighter.

THE COMPARISON TRAP

Comparison is something to be especially aware of when we are sharing our stories. It can easily sneak in and make camp in our hearts if we aren't on the lookout for it. It is a nasty game we play. If you want to find peace in your story and experience the joy of sharing it with others, comparison has to go. Think about it: Comparison is the source of jealousy, insecurity, dissatisfaction, self-pity, self-righteousness and bitterness. We certainly don't want these attitudes defining us, right?

We can notice differences between ourselves and others without falling into the trap of comparison. The danger, however, comes when we let ourselves create a hierarchy out of those differences. We each bring something special and unique to the table, and that's the way it's supposed to be. One of the best defenses I have found against comparison is celebration. When I start feeling pangs of comparison in my chest, I stop my thought-train in its tracks and back it up until I find my own insecurity. Once I know what causes the feelings of comparison, I am able to choose to set it aside for the time being and focus on the people I'm with, celebrating their journeys along with them. We are all doing the best we can with what we've been given, so instead of comparing and sizing each other up, we need to celebrate each other and lift each other up.

When I actively look for ways to admire and celebrate the people around me, I am a better and more Christ-like version of myself. My desire is to see more and more people choosing to speak up about the beautiful things we see in one another, with the confidence that our own worth is not compromised in doing so. Our differences give us unique wisdom and grace to share with others. When we celebrate those differences, we learn from each other. I don't want insecurity or confusion to dampen my perception of other people or the beautiful complexities and gifts the Lord has instilled in us. I want to cultivate relationships based on respect for others' strengths and differences, and find common ground in them. We can practice encouraging one another towards Christ through a perspective of celebration, rather than comparison.

Reflection Questions

1. What names for God stand out to you the most? Why do you think they stand out to you? What do these names mean to you?

2. What truths about your own identity stand out to you the most? Why? How do these truths affect how you see yourself?

3. What is your relationship with confidence? In what areas of life do you desire more confidence? How can the truths about God's character and your identity help you to find confidence?

4. What kinds of situations lead you into the trap of comparison? Instead of comparing, what would it look like to celebrate the differences you see in these situations?

CHAPTER TEN

Boundaries Don't Make You Cold

I'm not a very precise baker. I tend to estimate my measurements as I toss them in the bowl, and add extra ingredients as I see fit. I'm an expert at finding substitutions when food allergies come into play or when I simply don't have an ingredient on hand. One ingredient that I had always neglected in my baking was the pinch of salt required in most recipes. It just never seemed worth it, I guess. Why get out the salt if I'm just going to add a pinch? This was my practice—that is, until I tried my first cowboy cookie.

I'm sure not all cowboy cookies are created equal, but the ones I have tried are divine. When I worked downtown in Tucson, I used to treat myself to a latte from my favorite coffee shop, Cartel, nearly every Thursday. One Thursday, I decided to also get a cookie. I was intrigued by the name "cowboy cookie," and once I found out that it contained oatmeal, coconut and chocolate chips—three of my favorite baking ingredients—I was sold. I walked to my car with the little paper bag, imagining what the cookie would taste like, and took it out of the bag as soon as I was inside the car.

I took a bite, but was surprised by what I tasted. The taste was similar to what I had imagined, but much more intense, flavorful and mouth-watering. I took small bites after that first one, analyzing the flavor. *What was it that made this cookie taste so good?* Was it the type of chocolate? Sugar? Butter? I took another bite, and the lights turned on. *It was the salt.* The salt didn't come through as "salty" like I had always assumed it would in my own recipes. Rather, it punctuated the sweetness of the cookie, while making all the other flavors fuller.

It's common knowledge around the dinner table that salt brings out the flavor of other ingredients. I don't know why I had never made the connection to my baking before that cowboy cookie, but you had better believe that I now put salt into all my baking recipes—usually at least two pinches! When salt is in the right proportions, you almost forget it's there. Salt's job really isn't to be the dominate flavor; its job is to open up the array of flavors that make up your dish, whether it be pasta, asparagus or brownies.

BOUNDARIES ENHANCE VULNERABILITY'S GIFT

The way we use salt in baking is similar to how we use boundaries in sharing our stories. Like salt, boundaries help us to open up and share our experiences—our "flavors," if you will—more graciously with others. Boundaries communicate self-respect, self-knowledge, and self-control, which make the details you are willingly share feel like a gift. I've been in situations where

I've felt pressured to share more details than I've felt comfortable with in the name of transparency or "true friendship." I had no boundaries in place; so, consequently, I was hurt by sharing parts of my story with people who didn't deserve to hear them.

Often, in conversations about vulnerability and authenticity, it is assumed that in order to be vulnerable or authentic, you must also be transparent, as if withholding sensitive information is synonymous with lying. I don't think this is true at all. In fact, setting boundaries actually allows you to bring your most authentic self to the table. Boundaries allow you to open up your heart out of compassion, not out of pressure.

Sometimes, we feel like we need to share all the details of our stories in order for them to be effective or understood. Vulnerability is powerful and beautiful, but it is also a choice, and it should be treated that way. You should never feel forced or pressured to share more than you feel comfortable with. You can be honest and authentic with people without putting yourself into a potentially damaging situation. Your story is *your* story, and at the end of the day, it is up to you to choose how you share it with others. If you choose vulnerability, know that you are offering a very special gift. And if you choose to withhold in order to maintain your boundaries, know that your story is still incredibly powerful. Your willingness to share part of it is a testimony to God's grace in your life.

Brené Brown is a brilliant researcher and author who studies vulnerability, courage, shame and worthiness. In her book, *Rising Strong,* Brown shares that, within her research, a surprising relationship has emerged between boundaries and generosity. Generosity is a beautiful thing, especially in the form of vulnerability, but generosity without boundaries is a recipe for resentment.[1] She created a solution for navigating the issue of creating boundaries while still being generous with vulnerability, which she calls, "Living BIG: Boundaries, Integrity, and Generosity."[2]

At the crux of "Living BIG" is the question, *What boundaries do I need to put in place so I can work from a place of integrity and extend the most generous interpretations of intentions, words, and actions of others?*[3] This question shows that boundaries are twofold. We must put them in place so that we can share our story freely without putting ourselves in harm's way, but boundaries are also helpful in understanding how we can best meet the needs of others.

In the survey I conducted, some people described hesitation to share their stories because they had suffered abuse and were afraid of opening themselves up to being hurt again. This is understandable. I would never advocate that anyone put him- or herself in a potentially harmful situation. However, I found it amazing that the majority of the people who shared this sentiment were also the ones who seemed to know how powerful their stories were. They wanted to learn more about sharing their stories because they felt that they could help others. They made comments such as:

- People are not talking about this issue, but it's important.

- I know other people probably feel alone in this, just like I have felt.

- I know I could help others.

- I want to inspire others to overcome this type of struggle.

I think that this relationship, between pain and the use of that pain to reach out to others, is an interesting and beautiful one.

It says a lot about our desire as humans to connect and help others. It is a testament that God redeems, heals and restores, and that he calls us to do the same.

A TREASURE TO GIVE JOYFULLY

I can't help but think of sharing our stories as sharing our deepest treasures. They are so valuable, special and intimate. And as with giving any thoughtful gift, it is a joy to share our stories with others. I think of Paul's instructions to the Corinthians for how they ought to be giving. Let's walk through the passage of 2 Corinthians 9, and learn how to create appropriate boundaries while generously giving our treasure.

> "Therefore I considered it necessary to urge the brothers to go on ahead to you and arrange in advance the generous gift you promised, so that it will be ready as a gift and not as an extortion."[4]

Paul instructs the Corinthians to be prepared and ready with their gift so that when the time comes, they would be able to give joyfully, without being forced or pressured into giving. That is what we are able to do when we create boundaries for what we are willing to share and what we aren't willing to share. We are freed up to engage wholeheartedly in our conversations with others because we have control over what will be exposed. Boundaries keep us from giving into the pressure of oversharing in uncomfortable or overwhelming situations.

> "Remember this: The person who sows sparingly will also reap sparingly, and the person who sows generously will also reap generously. Each person should do as he has decided in his heart—not reluctantly or out of necessity, for God loves a

cheerful giver. And God is able to make every grace overflow to you, so that in every way, always having everything you need, you may excel in every good work. As it is written: He scattered; He gave to the poor; His righteousness endures forever."[5]

Sharing your story is a generous act. There are no set rules for how to share your story, but I think Paul's caution to the Corinthians—that those who sow sparingly will reap sparingly—rings true when it comes to sharing our stories, too. The more you are willing to step out of your comfort zone and open up your heart to others, the more opportunities you will have to see God work through you and your story. If you keep your story to yourself, you will never have the chance to see how it might encourage the people around you. However, Paul doesn't say, "In order to reap greatly, you must give everything you have to everyone around you." Rather, he instructs the Corinthians to seek the Lord for wisdom on how they ought to give, then do so from that conviction. Thus, the Corinthians could give with confidence and joy.

Likewise, seek wisdom from God about what to share, and with whom. He sees you, and he knows what's going on in your heart. He is the only one you need to please. After all, even if you only feel comfortable sharing a sliver of your story in this season, God is able to make every grace overflow to you. He will protect you and give you everything you need, whether you need the words to effectively share your story, or the words to politely decline.

"Now the One who provides seed for the sower and bread for food will provide and multiply your seed and increase the harvest of your righteousness. You will be enriched in every way for all generosity, which produces thanksgiving to God through us. For the ministry of this service is not only supplying the needs of the saints, but is also overflowing in many acts of thanksgiving to God."[6]

God is the one who makes all seeds grow. He can take your little nugget of hard-earned wisdom and multiply it in the heart of the person with whom you share it. God has given us great gifts, and when we share them with others, those gifts of grace increase in both the hearts of the giver and the receiver. What amazes me is that when we share our stories and give of our treasure generously, we actually create ways for God to be worshiped and glorified even more! When you encourage someone else, it creates thankfulness in their hearts, which results in praise to God—how neat is that?

> "They will glorify God for your obedience to the confession of the gospel of Christ, and for your generosity in sharing with them and with others through the proof provided by this service. And they will have deep affection for you in their prayers on your behalf because of the surpassing grace of God in you. Thanks be to God for His indescribable gift."[7]

I want people to say this about me: that I was obedient in sharing the gospel. I want to see more people in heaven because of my willingness to share my story, because I invited others into a relationship with Christ. I don't want to be ashamed or hold back words of encouragement when God has lavished so much grace upon me. May we always remember the riches we have in God's grace, and trust him with the opportunities we have to share our treasure with others.

TAKING OFF THE MASK

A topic that goes hand-in-hand with setting boundaries is that of embracing opportunities that may be outside of your comfort zone. When an occasion arises to share your story, it might feel intimidating or nerve-racking—even if it is well within the bounds you have decided. The personal and intimate nature of our stories makes sharing them a vulnerable act, even when we are prepared to share in a safe context.

Before moving away from home for my freshman year of college, my dad gave me one of the most bizarre gifts I have ever received. It was a big, furry, full-body gorilla costume. This costume was the real deal—it even came with rubbery gloves made to look like gorilla hands, and a furry head-mask with tiny slits to see through. I believe my dad accompanied his gift with the words, "I think you could make some good memories with this." It was random and hilarious, and I loved it. It didn't take me long to think of several potential uses for the gorilla costume, so I packed it in a storage bin that eventually found its place underneath the bed in my dorm room.

For the next couple of years, the gorilla costume stayed in that bin. I moved around to different rooms in different cities, but I always brought the gorilla costume with me—sliding the bin under my bed each time. Initially, when my dad first gave me that costume, I fully intended to use it to spook my friends or make a trip to Starbucks far more entertaining. But I never actually got around to it, and after a while, I forgot I even owned a gorilla costume.

Then, during my junior year of college, the perfect opportunity arrived to break out the gorilla suit. The campus Christian group I had been attending had planned a Halloween costume party at a nearby bowling alley. I didn't know very many people from the group at the time, and I didn't know if any of the girls I knew would attend. But I *did* know that this guy, Trevor (Remember him?), was going to the party, and that sealed the deal for me. I'm not one to make a scene or draw attention to myself, so wearing the gorilla suit felt like a bold move. But I talked myself into it by reassuring myself that no one would know who I was unless I told them, and I'd be able to "act natural" because no one would see my embarrassed face. Plus, I didn't want to show up at the party with a lame costume. From what I knew about Trevor, I figured that he would find a full-on gorilla costume funny, so I took my chances and entered the bowling alley, gorilla mask and all.

For the most part, my plan worked out pretty well. People loved the costume, and they thought it was funny that they couldn't figure out who was inside. Eventually, as the party wound down, Trevor and I ended up talking. I had been right; he loved the gorilla costume. So much so, that he had to know who was underneath. Perfect. This is what I had hoped for, right? It was the moment of truth—time to take off the mask and talk with Trevor, face-to-face. But instead of taking off the gorilla head with a cute "Surprise!" I panicked. Suddenly, the whole thing felt stupid. I was terrified that when he saw me, he would think I was a weird stalker who had dressed as a gorilla and come to the party just to talk to him for a couple of minutes.

Underneath the mask, I took a couple deep breaths. I could feel my face start to redden and sweat. *Great, now I'm the weird, blotchy and sweaty stalker,* I thought. I took a final breath and told myself, *It's going to be okay. No matter what happens, you're okay*—and I slipped off the mask. I will never forget the look of surprise and delight in Trevor's eyes when he recognized me. His laughter sent the warmest wave of relief over me. Instead of feeling exposed and awkward, I felt safe, accepted and valued. This memory, though silly and small, has been one of my greatest lessons in vulnerability and authenticity. I love looking back on that memory now that Trevor and I are married. It's a great reminder for me to "take off the mask" in other areas of my life, too.

To me, "taking off the mask" is a reminder to acknowledge my thoughts and feelings in moments of insecurity, and still choose to do the brave thing. It's a reminder that even when conversations are uncomfortable and I'm unsure how others will respond to me, showing up authentically—without a mask—is my best option. Sharing our stories with others is something that may always feel a little uncomfortable. But the willingness to step out of our comfort zones and be open with our lives allows for authentic, meaningful connections. It may not be easy, but it is worth the discomfort.

The fears I've held about sharing my story with others tend to come from confusion around the word "authenticity." Sometimes, the word "authentic" is thrown around and used in an idealistic way, rather than what the word actually means. If you look at how it's being used in culture, such as the very popular #liveauthentic hashtag on social media, you'll notice that the majority of pictures with that hashtag are staged, edited photos that do not reflect reality. In contrast, the definition of "authentic" is being true to one's own personality, spirit, or character.[8] When I talk about authenticity in this book, I am talking about that kind of authenticity—being true to the personality, spirit and character that God has blessed you with. With this perspective in mind, I think of taking off my mask not only as a practice of vulnerability, but as rooting my identity in truth. Every time I put myself out there, in big or small ways, I have an opportunity to recognize and validate my self-worth. This doesn't make taking off the mask any easier, per sé, but practicing it consistently has helped me to share my story more naturally.

The reality is, sharing our stories may never feel easy or comfortable. But if it were, where would the glory be? Think of an Olympic track runner—does she train so that the Olympic race will feel easy? Not a chance. Rather, she trains and practices the motions so many times that when the time comes for her to show her skill, her body is ready to work as hard as she can push it. I find this same benefit as I practice taking off the mask. It starts to become second-nature, our default. The more prepared we are to have honest, authentic conversations, the more opportunities we will have to share our stories in a way that transforms others.

HOW DO WE CREATE AUTHENTIC CONNECTIONS WITH PEOPLE?

As mentioned in earlier chapters, the Millennial generation is a generation that desires authenticity. This characteristic is often used to describe Millennials, and is seen as one of the more positive trends of the generation. An interesting phenomenon that supports this claim is the recent trend of "juice crawls" being favored over "bar crawls" by many Millennials.[9] A juice crawl is similar to a bar crawl: a group of people get together and travel from one bar to the next, sampling drinks. But in juice crawls, the drinks are various green juices and health tonics, instead of alcoholic drinks. What's interesting about this trend is that many of the young people interviewed about juice crawls explained that they preferred juice crawls because of the opportunity to connect with others in a more grounded, *authentic* way.[10] They were tired of the shallow, casual interactions happening in bars, where people drink too much alcohol and get drunk.

So aside from finding a local juice crawl, what are practical ways we can create authentic connections with others? This question may be easier to answer for some than others. Some people are wired to jump into thoughtful conversations and "get deep." They find it energizing and meaningful. On the other hand, there are the people who feel put off when they feel their personal space being invaded, and prefer to enter into heart-to-heart conversations on their own, measured terms. Neither of these tendencies is right or wrong, better or worse—they are just different. I bet you can guess on which side you tend to fall. Knowing your own personality will help you find ways to engage and connect with others that are authentic to you. If sitting in a quaint coffee shop with a friend for hours isn't your thing, that's okay. God gave you the personality, spirit and character he did on purpose, and there are plenty of people who need the exact mixture that you have to offer. Maybe you ask a co-worker to join you on a walk to get lunch? Or invite a new friend to go cycling or hiking? There is no need to plan the start of a spiritual conversation. Rather, by simply inviting others into your life, you will have more opportunities for those conversations to take place.

Though we desire authentic interactions, we need to keep in mind that the only variable we can control is ourselves. We can't make others open up to us, or even persuade them to. But we can model vulnerability ourselves, which might give others the comfort to do the same. Deep conversations are also not something we can just dive into any time we want to feel something meaningful. That would be the opposite of authenticity, right? Engaging in authentic interactions needs to be a practice woven into our bones. This is why it's so important to root our identities in Christ and know our stories. It helps us to let go of all the questions and searching and measuring up, which makes us free to be ourselves, confident in where we've come from and where we're going. That's what the Millennials at the juice crawl were looking for when they said they wanted to meet grounded and authentic people. People are searching for a grounding force in their lives, be it through exercise, meditation or diet. What an opportunity we have to demonstrate the grounded-ness that comes through hope in Christ and peace with God!

WHEN SHARING ABOUT HURT CAUSED BY OTHERS

There are many ways our hearts can be hurt in this life, whether from loss or letdowns. How we choose to handle that pain will have a big impact on our stories. But there is one type of pain that is especially important to consider when we are sharing our stories: pain caused by others. It's a sensitive aspect of our story, because the people who hurt us most are usually the people we love and trust most. Dealing with the reality of pain caused by another person, whether intentional or not, can be difficult to wrap our heads around. Many questions arise when we try to reconcile our feelings of pain and love, trust and distrust. Oftentimes, we don't give ourselves enough time to work through those inevitable questions, which can lead to unfortunate consequences.

From what I know about myself and others, we usually hop quickly into one of two boats when we are hurt by someone. Either we take the position of a victim, or we take the responsibility, blaming ourselves for hurt caused by someone else. We usually set sail on whichever boat we choose, and go full-speed ahead. What we don't usually realize is that both of these options head to the same destination—one of bitterness, helplessness and deep insecurity. I've jumped on both boats at different times in my life, and have stayed aboard each of them long enough to know that they don't take you anywhere you want to go.

I think we jump so quickly into these boats because we are trying to make sense of what happened. Absolutes are always more appealing than vague unknown or murky uncertainty. We like to know who is to blame and why we were hurt. We try to control the situation right away, by telling ourselves a simplified story of what happened. But even if these simplified stories feel accurate at the time, we'll be disillusioned if we hold onto them for too long.

We will be stuck, miles from shore, miles from safety, healing, and wholeness. The simple stories often aren't what they seem, and when people are involved, the reality is never as simple as black-or-white, yes-or-no, stay-or-leave.

If we are to find healing in this life, we need to face our hurt inflicted by others. We need to be willing to let go of our simple stories and find a way to accept the complexities that come with human relationships. That means finding a way to incorporate our hurt into our stories in a way that is honest, for both ourselves and the people who have harmed us. The thing about hurt is that it never ends the story; it either changes the story or begins a new one.

If you're hurting now, it might seem impossible that the pain you're feeling will ever subside. It will, in time; but until it does, rest in the truth that God is with you, wrapping his arms around you. "The Lord is near the brokenhearted; He saves those crushed in spirit."[11] We all have our own ways of mourning the losses that break our hearts. Whether or not someone hurt us intentionally, we need to give ourselves the time and space necessary to heal. With healing comes renewed compassion and forgiveness for those that hurt us, and compassion is the voice we should listen to when we share our stories of hurt caused by others.

Each of us needs to decide for ourselves how we will handle sharing our hurt caused by other people. My best piece of advice to help you answer that question for yourself is to treat your story as a gift that you offer to your listener. If you are sharing your story to empathize, encourage or find common ground, it is an act of grace. And if it is an act of grace, resentment and bitterness should not be ingredients tossed into your story. There are several ways we can share our stories without defaming others, and following these approaches can lead to even greater healing in our own lives. I have formed a list of questions that I ask myself before sharing a story that involves someone else. I think of these questions as a strainer. Each time I'm about to write or talk about a hurtful experience with another person, I filter my memories, feelings and words through the following questions to make sure my heart is in the right place.

WHAT IS MY REASON FOR SHARING THIS STORY?

This is the most important question to ask yourself. *Why am I sharing this now? Why am I sharing it with this person?* Is it out of empathy, to let a friend or group of people know, "Hey, I understand you; I've been there myself too."? Or is it out of the contempt or bitterness you still feel towards the person who hurt you? There is a time and a place for every story. Willingness to be vulnerable with our own hurt and experience is key, but it is unwise to spread stories out of bitterness that may smear another person's reputation.

WOULD SHARING THIS STORY BE SELF-INDULGENT?

This question can be quite humbling at times. Be honest with yourself. Are you hoping to be pitied, let off the hook, or even seen as valiant for overcoming such hurt or circumstances? If so, press the pause-button and wait for a more appropriate time to share this part of your story.

On the other hand, if you have come to a point in your journey where you have been able to forgive and move on from the hurt, sharing your experience might not be self-indulgent at all. Rather, it might be a situation to which others can relate, and you can root your story in the desire to inspire hope in others as they overcome the hurt in their own lives.

ARE THERE OTHER WAYS TO COMMUNICATE MY HURT?

Once I get to this question, I usually have some sort of breakthrough. The lights turn on, and suddenly, I am able to learn from my own story. Because here's the thing we've got to keep in mind: as Christians, our stories are not actually about us. They're about God. And so, when we share about events or circumstances in our lives, we should be looking for ways to reflect him and his character, even when we are feeling hurt.

It's possible that you don't even need to share the exact events of what happened, or the people who played a part, in order to communicate the message of your story powerfully. Try narrowing your story down to how you felt, what you were thinking, what you learned or how you grew from it. People can connect with those ideas without the specific details. Answering these questions will reveal what still needs healing and what has already been healed.

AM I SHARING MY STORY, OR SOMEONE ELSE'S?

This little piece of wisdom is so important when sharing your story. Don't speak for other people, or try to explain their motives or intentions. Just tell your story, and tell it truthfully.

Reflection Questions

1. What comes to mind when you think of boundaries? Do you see them as positive or negative? How have you created or maintained boundaries in the past?

2. What boundaries do you think would be healthy when sharing your particular story?

3. Do you agree with the idea that setting boundaries can help you to share your story more joyfully? Why or why not?

4. When have you "taken off the mask" in front of others? What happened? What did you learn from the experience?

Part Three

SHARE YOUR STORY

CHAPTER ELEVEN

Finding Common Ground

Just west of downtown Tucson sits Tumamoc Hill. When I first moved to Tucson, Tumamoc Hill was one of the places that people repeatedly suggested I check out. They said it was a great hike—short and intense, but with beautiful views of the city at the top. It seemed everyone had a story about Tumamoc Hill. Some people told me about the perfect sunset they saw from the top, others about their first attempt at running up the path. One friend even told me that she once did the whole hike in flip-flops, which sounded painful. Each story was different, and most people shared something unpleasant about the hike, like how shaky their legs were, how hot it was or how many rattlesnakes they almost stepped on. However, one thing they all had in common was their sincerity as they would tell me, "You just need to go."

I finally agreed to take their advice. At first glance, Tumamoc Hill didn't strike me as anything too special. It looked like the rest of the foothills at the base of the Tucson Mountains. From a distance, I could distinguish several radio and television transmitters at the top. As I got closer, I saw a few scattered buildings about halfway up the hill, owned by the University of Arizona and used for research. It seemed like a place that would have a big fence around it, with warnings posted against trespassing and a locked gate for qualified personnel.

But when I turned onto the road alongside the base of Tumamoc Hill, I realized that it was quite the opposite. There was a paved trail leading from the base of the hill to the very top. It was filled with a steady stream of people. The trail curved its way to the top, making the upward hike about a mile and a half long. The elevation gain was about 750 feet—not necessarily spectacular, but it sure felt significant as I pounded my way up in the Arizona sun.

Now that I've experienced it myself, I've become one of those people telling others, "You just need to go." In the two years that I've lived in Tucson, Tumamoc Hill has become one of my favorite places. It's a place I can go for a fun date with Trevor, a place I can go to remind myself that I can do hard things, and a place that I can go with an anxious, restless mind, knowing that by the time I make it to the top and down again, I'll have a new perspective on my situation.

And what I think makes it so special isn't the fact that it's a hill, or that it's a work-out to hike up, or that it's (kind of) in the wilderness. Rather, I think it has to do with that steady stream of people making their way up and down Tumamoc Hill. You see all types on that path. You see moms and dads pushing strollers, and you see kindergarteners running at the start, only to be later found on their parents' shoulders. You see old men with white hair, running the hill multiple times in a row. There are obese people and fit people, pregnant women, people wearing weighted backpacks and ankle cuffs, people of all colors speaking various languages. Different people, each with a different background—but in that moment on the hill, they're all in it together.

I can't count how many times I've been encouraged by someone else on that hill, whether it's from watching a man persevere up the steepest part of the hill, or when a stranger goes out of her way to cheer me on with a "Good work!" I've been given advice on my running form by a sweet, small, white-haired man who ran the hill three times in a row, while wearing a gold medal from a race he won "in his prime." One of my favorite memories on this hill is the time that I happened to be keeping pace with a group of moms, who all got together every Sunday to walk and chat. They invited me into their conversation, and we decided to challenge ourselves to run the rest of the way to the top, laughing most of the way.

What I love about Tumamoc Hill is that it makes me conscious of both the uniqueness of each of us on the path and our commonalities. We each have our own set of circumstances, and the hike is definitely more difficult for some than others. But when we're out there on the path, making our way up that hill, we can each relate to one another's immediate situation. We feel the burn in one another's legs. We know the shortness of breath; we know how difficult it can be to gather enough breath to cheer another on. But we do it—because we remember a time when we were the ones who wouldn't have made it if it weren't for someone else sparing a bit of their oxygen to tell us, "You're doing great." We find encouragement in the blessed souls who have already made it up and pass us on their way down. We see that they made it, which helps us find the resolve to make it, too. There's nothing better than hearing someone say, "You can do it; you're almost there!" For the hikers on Tumamoc Hill, the hill becomes our literal common ground.

HOW DO WE FIND COMMON GROUND?

The idea of finding common ground with people of other faiths or no faith may feel threatening to some Christians. You may feel like you would have to compromise on your beliefs or soften the gospel to find common ground. Finding common ground can definitely be touchy, that's for sure. And it is a topic that requires much wisdom to handle correctly.

But the times I have let my guard down to seek common ground have been opportunities for me to share the gospel in its truest form. When it comes down to it, some of my most meaningful conversations have occurred when I have taken down my barriers, hushed my judgments and simply listened as a friend who cares. Not so that I could eventually prove someone wrong or point out holes in her beliefs, but because she was hurting, confused or afraid, and just needed someone she could trust to help carry her burden.

That is common ground. It's the willingness to not only acknowledge pain, but enter into it for the sake of a loved one. It's the courage to say, "Hey, you're not alone in this. I know it doesn't make sense. It hurts, but this is not the end." Or, "Me, too. It's hard. But no matter how hard it gets, we're going to make it out together." These words speak volumes about our love and care for others, which are powerful enough to break down barriers. Using opportunities like these to communicate love is how we build trust. When trust is the underlying foundation in a relationship, you are able to share your beliefs and perspectives from a place of understanding.

DON'T FORFEIT BEFORE YOU TRY

When we see someone hurting or recognize that someone is struggling with a situation, it may be natural to respond with empathy. We might approach this person and ask if she wants to talk, or offer our help in another way. These are kind acts of love that build a bridge of trust. However, as followers of Christ, we have more to offer than a shoulder to cry on or a surprise venti latte. We have the hope of Jesus Christ—the healer of broken bones and broken hearts alike. Why is it so much harder to offer Jesus to those in need than to offer a hug or a casserole?

This question echoes one that I had asked in my survey. I had asked people to share what kept them from bringing God up in their conversations. By far, the most common response was that they didn't want to make others uncomfortable. Now, I can totally relate to that feeling. I can't even count the times that I have held back from explaining my beliefs or asking a spiritual question, only because I assumed that doing so would kill the conversation, or maybe even drive a wedge in a relationship.

To be fair, this fear is completely valid. There is always a chance that sharing your beliefs or spiritual experiences will make someone else uncomfortable. We have no guarantee that every spiritual conversation will be comfortable for the other person or for you. That being said, we also need to take an honest look at the assumptions driving our fear. Fear can manifest itself in our thoughts in some of the following ways:

- I'm afraid that I will push this person away.

- What if something I say turns someone off to the Gospel?

- I'm afraid that I'll mess up what God wants me to say.

- What if this person think I'm just another hypocrite?

- I don't want to push people away or pressure them.

Do these thoughts sound familiar to you? I imagine that you can relate to at least one, if not all of these feelings. Why do we assume that speaking about religion will cause discomfort? My guess is that for many of us, the method we were taught to use in sharing the gospel or talking about God with our friends is hard to reconcile in a society that values pluralism. One of the side effects of this conflict is that sharing our faith or helping someone spiritually may feel like the ultimate form of judgment. When we offer the gospel to our friends, we might be misunderstood as being close-minded, so we hold back from sharing the hope we have in Christ because it doesn't seem politically correct.

This phenomenon of withholding our greatest treasure from those we love is a widespread issue among Christians today. People who are hurting are usually the most receptive to the gospel. That's why Jesus focused so much of his ministry on the poor, brokenhearted and downtrodden. That's why he called us to live our lives in the same way! The broken are the most desperate for connection, meaning and hope. Why do we shy away from opportunities to meet them in their greatest need, and offer the healing grace of the gospel?

Bruce Gilson, a pastor at Gateway Church in Austin, Texas addressed this problem in a recent sermon to his congregation. I found his words so poignant and convicting. He says,

> Some of us work in offices where no one really knows how important our faith is to us. Some of us sit in offices next to people who have gone through a brutal divorce, or they are having trouble with their teenage kid and don't know where

to turn for answers. Some of us have neighbors who have gone through a miscarriage or who got laid off from their jobs. Some of us have buddies who just lost a parent. And we see the pain in their eyes. And maybe we pat them on the shoulder, maybe we mumble an "I'm sorry", maybe we write a note, "If there is anything I can do, let me know." But we're silent about the one thing in our lives that we are most sure about.[1]

Why do we assume that sharing the gospel will push others away? This question has stumped me for some time. My best guess is that the fear of pushing others away exists because we weren't taught to share the gospel in a personal, meaningful way. But what if we rethought our approach to how we share the gospel or explain our faith to others? What if sharing our faith was more about connecting with others, finding common ground and explaining our personal experiences, rather than trying to convince them that Jesus is the answer to their problems? I'm sure that this would communicate more love than judgment. I'm also sure that it would open doors instead of close them. In fact, I know it would, because every time I've tried sharing my faith in this way, it has.

After all, Jesus called us to be known by our love, didn't he?[2] We communicate love when we are sincere, patient and gentle. We communicate love when we ask questions, and really listen to what's being said in response. We communicate love when we offer a perspective that may help a friend in need. We communicate love when we tell our friend that we care about her, and that we want her to experience the same hope, peace, strength and joy that we have found. We communicate love when we share the gospel with both boldness and gentleness; boldness coming from our unwavering faith and gentleness from the wisdom God gives us to relate the gospel in a personal way.

TAKE THE PRESSURE OFF

One Wednesday night at youth group, a girl in my small group, Janelle, brought up this exact fear. She told us how one of her friends, who is not a Christian, had been on her heart recently. Janelle explained that their friendship had always been relatively light and casual, but recently, their conversations had been giving way to deeper topics. Janelle confessed that she had recognized opportunities to bring up spiritual ideas or ask her friend about her beliefs, but she held back. "I just didn't want to make her uncomfortable," Janelle said.

I was already working on this section of this book, so I was extremely interested in how the other girls in the group would respond to Janelle. There were some knowing sighs and nods from the group, and then Janelle said this golden phrase: "Well, really, I'm afraid that *I'll* be uncomfortable." How true and transparent! Isn't that what's really going on in all of our hearts? Even when our concern for our friend's comfort might be genuine, how often is it multiplied by our own fear of discomfort?

Janelle's acknowledgement of her own discomfort and decision to share it with the group was so beautiful and brave. It's difficult to admit when we are holding back, especially within a group of people who keep us accountable. But if we want to be Christ-followers who represent Christ in powerful ways, we're going to need to be open, brave and uncomfortable.

The encouraging thing about choosing to be open, brave and uncomfortable is that it gets much easier the more we try. As we step out into the unknown of wandering spiritual conversations, we realize that despite all the pressure we may feel, we are not capable of winning any hearts or making someone believe in Jesus. That's God's job, as the Holy Spirit opens people's hearts with conviction and wisdom. The more we trust in Jesus to do his part, the more we discover what our own is. The more we obey and do our part, the more we see Jesus do his. It's a beautiful, life-changing exchange.

WE ARE CALLED TO BE BRAVE

When I started reading the Bible for myself, I was blown away by how much I recognized myself in the people of the Bible. I had grown up hearing the stories, and was familiar with most of them, but Moses, Daniel, Esther, David, Paul and Peter never seemed like real people with thoughts, feelings, motives and fears like me. Instead, they seemed like flat, hard-to-relate-to caricatures. So when I read of Moses begging God to send someone else to lead the Israelites out of Egypt because he didn't think he was a good public speaker,[3] or Sarah laughing when God told her she would become pregnant in her old age,[4] or Joseph leaving the room to cry when he saw all of his brothers,[5] or King Solomon describing love in his poems,[6] or Daniel displaying commitment to God long before he ended up in the lion's den,[7] or Jonah waiting to see Nineveh destroyed after he prophesied to them,[8] or David writing of his emotional highs and lows, loneliness and adultery[9] —I was hooked. This list is just the very tip of the iceberg. But the point is that the people we read about in the Bible were real people—just like you and me. When I realized that, I realized that God could use me in the same mighty ways that he used them.

Following Jesus and obeying his call to share the good news with the lost is never about feeling like we've got it all together. Rather, it's about acknowledging that we don't have it all together, but knowing that Jesus holds us and pieces our broken hearts back together. It can be awkward and uncomfortable to let our guard down and take off our masks, but it's so worth it. We are called to be brave and rely on the strength and wisdom of the Lord, are we not? Think about Joshua, for example. The Lord called him to lead the Israelites into the Promised Land, and he was terrified, unsure of himself and doubtful that anyone would take him seriously. After all, he had to take the place of Moses. And instead of removing Joshua's insecurities doubts with a quick-fix, God kept reminding him, "Be strong and courageous. Be strong and courageous. I will be with you; I won't forsake you."[10] Over and over again, God reminded Joshua of his presence, calling him to trust and be brave. And you know what happened over time? Joshua became a distinguished, brave leader of Israel.

That's what I pray each of us will be able to say one day. That despite the fears we've had and the insecurities we've faced, we staked our trust in the Lord, and obeyed him by bravely following where he led. If we live this way, we will bear fruit.

WHAT IF I CAN'T ANSWER THEIR QUESTIONS?

From the very beginning, God has been all about giving his people the words they needed to carry out his work. We see a great example of this in the story of Moses. God explained Moses' mission, and he told Moses exactly what he wanted him to say. God literally gave Moses a script, a word-for-word message for him to bring to the elders. But it didn't take long before Moses doubted if God had fully equipped him. He turned to God and asked a question I'm sure I would have asked, too: "What if they do not believe me or listen to me and say, 'The Lord did not appear to you'?"[11]

God responded to his question by performing a couple of miracles to demonstrate that he was completely capable of fulfilling the work to which he had called Moses. The miracles were vivid, and quite terrifying—like turning a rod into a snake and momentarily covering one of Moses' hands with leprosy.

Understandably overwhelmed, Moses decided to remind God that he isn't the most articulate speaker—maybe God should choose someone else to do the speaking. This too, sounds all too familiar to me. *Um, no thanks, God; I don't think I'd be able to relate very well to that person. Or, Lord, I'd love to share the gospel with her, but I just don't think I know enough; I probably wouldn't be able to answer all her questions.*

And for that excuse, God had quite the response. He answered Moses, "Who gave human beings their mouths? Who makes them deaf or mute? Who gives them sight or makes them blind? Is it not I, the Lord? Now go; I will help you speak and will teach you what to say."[12] Yet even after God spoke to Moses and promised to give him the words *and* the help he needed to speak them, Moses *still* wouldn't rise to the challenge. He begged the Lord to send someone else. And you know what happened? *God sent someone else.* He called Aaron, Moses' brother to do the speaking for Moses. But this was not without consequences. God's anger burned against Moses for this.[13] Moses trusted God, but only up to a limit. Yes, God provided a way out for Moses, but it wasn't without a great cost. Moses' fear and stubbornness led him to disobedience as he denied the work to which God had called him.

I'm thankful for the story of Moses, and that his story continues long after this instance at the burning bush. Moses learned along the way, and he became better at obeying God. He experienced so many miracles, and God used him in amazing ways as the Israelites left Egypt and wandered in the desert. He spoke with the Lord, one-on-one, and was so close to God's glory, that when he came down from Mount Sinai, he had to wear a veil over his face so he wouldn't blind the Israelites. That's an amazing, beautiful picture of redemption.

Whether you relate to Moses more in his stubbornness or in his leadership, know that there is always hope and opportunity to turn back to God and trust his plan for your life. I challenge you to write down the fears or hesitations that prevent you from opening up to share your story with others, then give them over to God. Ask him to teach you to be brave and bold so that you don't forfeit your opportunities to share the Gospel with people who badly need it.

Reflection Questions

1. Think of a time when someone went out of their way to offer you support or encouragement. How did this make you feel? What can you learn from it?

2. Can you think of a time you neglected to share your hope with a loved one when they were hurting? If so, how did you feel afterwards? How does this impact how you will approach similar situations in the future?

3. Do you relate to Moses in his stubbornness to trust God? What excuses do you offer when you feel the Lord leading you to uncomfortable situations?

4. We can use evidence of God's faithfulness in the past to combat our fears about sharing the gospel with others. Where do you see this evidence in the Bible? What about in your own life?

CHAPTER TWELVE

Listen First, Then Create Dialogue

Listening is the first step towards creating open conversations about beliefs and faith. It is important that we listen well if we hope to engage in dialogue on the grounds of understanding and respect. This is a cornerstone practice in any communication field, and we'd do well to take a play from that playbook. In order to create effective communication, we need to look at our audience and their needs before addressing them. We need to do our best to understand their perspective so that we can make our own understood in a respectful way. I have learned the hard way that if I am not willing to do the work of understanding the people with whom I communicate, my message is bound to break down—no matter how compelling or attractive it may be. If we hope to influence the world for Christ through our stories, we need to put in the time to not just understand our own stories, but also understand the people we hope to reach. I have found that the more I seek to understand others and their point of view, the greater grace and empathy I have for them. Grace and empathy are two key ingredients to sharing a message that moves people.

The focus of this chapter is the idea of dialogue. By dialogue, I mean the practice of both listening and contributing to the larger conversations happening in our world today. There is so much uncertainty in our world, and many hard questions are being asked in regards to human rights, social justice and environmental issues. These conversations are complex, but we should not shy away from them or throw our hands up in defeat. Rather, as God's people, we ought to press into these issues deeper, beyond the surface level. By using your story to reconcile your faith with some of these issues, you will be equipped to speak to them from your personal experience, while also expressing your hope in Christ.

One of the marks of the Millennial generation is their humanitarian investment. Millennials are a generation of action-takers and do-gooders. If we are informed about and involved in the shaping of cultural conversation, we will have opportunities to display Christ as a very real solution to many of the issues facing our world. How we choose to engage in these conversations will greatly affect the way non-Christians view Christianity and God.

Racial tensions, poverty, refugee crises, homelessness, LGBTQ rights, sex-trafficking, climate change; these are just the tip of the iceberg when it comes to the humanitarian issues our world is trying to navigate. Lists of one problem after another can be overwhelming. They may even make you want to check out a bit. Approaching all these "issues" with a wide-angle lens can make it hard to identify where, or how, you fit in to make a difference.

It's like the difference between learning about six-thousand hungry people in your city versus learning about a person who needs a meal right around the corner from your house. Knowing about the six-thousand hungry people might fan your desire to help, but that number is so intimidating that you might not know where to start. In this case, nothing is done, and the need eventually slips from your mind. On the other hand, if you hear about *one* person near your house who needed a meal, you could find a way to meet that need. You might bring them an extra plate from your own family's dinner. You might invite them to your house for a meal, or just stop by the store and pick up some food that would nourish them.

As we discuss different issues and opportunities for finding common ground within today's culture, I challenge you to focus on the issues that especially resonate in your heart. I believe that God molds and bends each of our hearts in different ways to reflect his own. The suffering people in the crises mentioned above—refugees, victims of sexual assault, kids in the foster care system, and so many others—each break God's heart, and he calls his children in different ways to meet those needs in his name. I don't know your specific circumstances or what needs particularly move you, so I will maintain a "big-picture" perspective for the remainder of this chapter. But as we discuss our opportunities for common ground within humanitarian efforts or politics, consider how your story might help you to engage in dialogue around the issues for which God has given you the most passion.

HUMANITARIAN EFFORTS

One of the most positive attributes of Christians' reputations is their ability to rise up and meet the needs of others during times of crisis. Caring for the poor, sick, marginalized and alien has been part of our call from the very beginning. Long before there were any government-organized humanitarian relief programs in place, faith communities have found ways to assist people afflicted by natural disaster, persecution, uprooting and war.[1] Monasteries and churches have long been seen as a place of refuge and charity to the poor or stranger. Christians, whether inspired individually or mobilized through their church community, have often been the driving force behind advocacy and public awareness of humanitarian efforts. Our history and impact in situations such as tsunami relief, orphan care and tending to marginalized elderly people provides Christians with credibility in conversations about human crisis.[2]

What experiences have you had serving on behalf of the afflicted? Your personal examples of serving and doing good on behalf of others can help you to start conversations around universal needs. Dialogue can take place when you share your personal stories, observations and growth, and invite others to share about their experiences with you. They may have different motivations or perspectives for their humanitarian works, but you can find common ground in the shared effort of relieving another's suffering.

This may be tricky to navigate if your only experiences serving have been driven explicitly by evangelism. While there are many secular groups who celebrate the aid that churches provide in communities locally and across the world, there can also be strong opposition when Christians disrespect the beliefs of others or involve themselves in situations purely to elicit conversions. So how do we engage in healthy dialogue when these oppositions may be targeted at us?

Let's look at an organization that has navigated these questions well for a long time. World Vision International (World Vision) is a Christian humanitarian aid and development organization that was founded in 1950. Originally, it was created to meet emergency needs of missionaries in the field. As time went on, World Vision began partnering directly with communities to develop sustainable success in health care, agriculture, education, poverty relief, clean water and gender equality. Today, World Vision is active in over 90 countries and is recognized as a leading organization in humanitarian relief by Christians, non-Christians and governments alike. Despite World Vision's growth and the support it has garnered across religious lines, the organization has stayed deeply committed to its Christian roots. Their approach to humanitarian aid is wholly influenced by Jesus, and they do not try to hide or soften that fact. World Vision's website includes a statement of their beliefs:

> Our faith in Jesus Christ is core to who we are. As an expression of God's unconditional love for all people, especially vulnerable children, we serve alongside the poor and oppressed. We hope to live as followers of Christ by being active, visible bearers of God's love.
>
> Relying on God's grace and Spirit, we affirm the truth of the gospel and our hope in Christ through our character, speech, actions, and in the signs of God's power at work in individual lives, in the communities where we work, and in all creation.[3]

How has World Vision gained so much respect in the eyes of people outside of the church? There are certainly a lot of factors at play here. Consistency, for one. Not only has World Vision been dedicated to meeting needs and providing relief since 1950, but they have also demonstrated the impact of sustained development and long-term relief support. Examples of these include World Vision's leadership in caring for Vietnamese refugees in the 1970s and their agricultural development during the Ethiopian famine of the 1980s.[4] The consistency of World Vision has allowed them to have an obvious global impact, which has spurred additional support for their services.

For example, in 2015 alone, World Vision provided aid for over twelve million disaster survivors and refugees, provided clean water in communities for over two million people and helped to created 1.6 million jobs in developing countries.[5] While all of these achievements were inspired by Jesus, the organization's acceptance and inclusion of those outside of the Christian faith has given them sway and influence in conversations about humanitarian aid at the international level. World Vision has committed to respect and work together with people of differing beliefs and religions. They explain their approach to engaging people outside of the Christian faith:

> In our work among people of other world religions, we value our common humanity and common desire to care for and protect vulnerable children. By developing relationships with people of other faiths, we have found that suspicion, mistrust, and fear are replaced with trust, friendship, and mutual support.[6]

We can learn from World Vision's example. While our motivations for good works and service may be rooted in Christ, we do not need to conduct all our good works in a strictly Christian context. In fact, doing so separates us from the larger conversation. Rather, we can celebrate the good work others are doing, regardless of their religious affiliation. We can join forces with people and organizations working to meet needs and promoting justice for the afflicted. In doing so, we find common ground and a place for dialogue in our shared compassion for humanity. And as we cheer others on and honor their work and stories, we have license to share our own stories.

POLITICS

Now, here's a topic that will likely either make your eyes light up or make you cringe: politics. Politics can be touchy, that's for sure. In fact, politics is probably the hardest area to create dialogue around because it tends to polarize people, even when religious affiliations are not addressed. Despite the difficulties of political discussions, it's important that we consider our role in the conversation. We are entering the conversation following a long history of Christian activism. Some of the political efforts Christians have historically championed are seen as very positive, while some are viewed as hypocritical or even extremist.[7] This provides us, as Christ-followers, with ample opportunities to offer new perspectives as we engage in political dialogue. Politics is an especially relevant topic for dialogue and sharing your personal story, since many Millennials—62% of non-Christians and 47% of Christians—believe that conservative Christians in politics are a significant problem facing America today.[8] We should be looking for more opportunities to find common ground, rather than polarize each other.

When it comes to politics, the conversation can be easily muddied with stark stereotypes and assumptions. The best thing you can do to create dialogue around political topics is dismantle the stereotypes you hold yourself. Step outside of the hard boundaries of party lines, and consider where you, yourself, stand on certain issues. Which policies do you think will have the greatest benefit to humankind? Why?

When you answer these questions based on your own reasoning, story and convictions, you will be better equipped to engage in fruitful conversations with others. Likewise, you will better understand the opinions others have chosen for themselves, having done the work yourself. And hopefully, you will be able to respect their perspectives, even when they differ from your own.

Much like Jesus motivates Christian action in humanitarian efforts, he ought to guide us in political engagement, as well. But following Jesus as our influence does not mean that we need to prove our political points through theology. For example, quoting Scripture as "proof" for a political stance isn't very effective with people who don't believe the Bible to be the living Word of a real God. Of course, the Bible should influence your political reasoning, but using it as the only justification for your perspective doesn't offer an invitation for discussion or an entry point for common ground. In their book *Good Faith*, authors David Kinnaman and Gabe Lyons address the tendency to offer theological answers to political questions. I found their distinction between the two to be incredibly helpful:

> Our theology should not be divorced from our politics, but we need to be clear about which is which. Theology is our best understanding of God's revelation. Politics is about making wise and prudent decisions in a particular context. Theological reflection can and must inform our politics, but let's also acknowledge that Christians in other contexts may come to different political conclusions after their own process of theological reflection.[9]

Political engagement is important because of the significant impact it will have on human lives. If we don't partake in the conversation meaningfully, we give up the opportunity to represent Jesus' heart in political issues. If you'd like to read a biblical example of someone who intentionally and respectfully engaged in politics, check out the story of Daniel.[10] He remained faithful to God, even in a godless civilization. He gained influence in society through his integrity and intelligence, which opened up the opportunity to offer his God-given wisdom in the form of advice to the Babylonian king. May we cultivate God's heart and wisdom in our political context as we influence the culture in godly ways.

COMMON GROUND STARTS AND ENDS WITH LOVE

The practice of finding common ground is generous and full of grace. It honors the person you are speaking to as you seek his or her viewpoints and interpretations. By asking questions and genuinely listening to your friend's answers, you will gain respect in her eyes. Later, if you choose to offer your own interpretation as an alternative, they will be more likely to take the time to thoroughly consider your words. Authenticity is powerful. When you demonstrate your interest and investment in another as a person, not a project, your words will automatically carry more weight in his or her heart. There is no doubt that, at times, this model of sharing your story and explaining your faith will lead to difficult conversations. There will be times when you won't have answers or feel comfortable. In these situations, it will be tempting to either run away or become defensive, both of which would communicate disinterest in an open conversation after all.

Instead of alienating non-believers by highlighting the differences between our worldviews or beliefs, why not first seek connection in the areas we do have agreement? I'm not saying that we shouldn't share our opinions or explain why we believe something to be true. In fact, I believe we *should* be sharing and explaining, rather than debating or assuming others' thoughts.

The practice of finding common ground was first demonstrated to us by God himself. Not only did he create us, but he made us to be in relationship with him. How would your interactions change if you followed that example? What if, as a church, we listened, understood and related to others through our own similar experiences? That common ground could open up a door to introduce others to the hope and promise of a relationship with Christ.

Reflection Questions

1. How does your faith and relationship with God inform your engagement with the larger conversations about social issues in today's culture?

2. Are there any humanitarian efforts near to your heart that you think the Lord could use to help you find common ground with non-believers? What is the first step you could take to develop relationships in that sphere?

3. How could you wisely integrate your theological and political views? In what areas do you see room for improvement as you explain your political views to people with other faiths or backgrounds?

4. What role can you play in improving the way the church communicates and engages with people outside of the church?

CHAPTER THIRTEEN

Engaging in Dialogue with Grace

There is a village in the Yucatán Peninsula of Mexico named San Francisco, and it is very dear to my heart. In that village, a church congregation meets together in a large Mayan hut. I have been blessed to witness this church grow from its very beginning. The church in Grand Rapids that I had grown up in has partnered with local missionaries in San Francisco for many years, and I had the joy of serving alongside of them throughout high school and college on yearly mission trips. I was there the day the San Francisco church building was dedicated. On that day, the church community hosted a beautiful service and celebration, followed by a prayer walk around the village. As we walked, our team, alongside local church members, sang different songs in Spanish and Maya, including the lyrics, "They will know we are Christians by our love." At first, singing that song felt powerful and hopeful. I looked around, and saw the very tangible fruit of God transforming lives. It was only a few years before when these people first heard about Jesus' love and salvation. Now, we were walking together through their village, praying that God would move even more hearts.

As we walked along, I was holding a little boy named Juan on my hip. Juan, affectionately known as Juancito, was five years old, but so small that he felt like a toddler. Juancito was packed full of energy; he was always running around and seeking attention from those around him. His voice was always loud, shrill and excited. He had a volatile mood; at times, he would storm away pouting in anger, only to turn around and charge at me, giving me the best bear-hug his little arms could manage. But something must have changed in his heart during that prayer walk. For once, he was totally at peace in my arms, even singing the songs along with us.

Even in that moment of beauty, I doubted God's ability to use me. I questioned my competence and ability to reflect Jesus. As an American in a developing village, I wondered if the interest and love shown to me by the people in San Francisco stemmed only from my foreign status, or if they were truly attracted to the Jesus they saw in me. I wondered if God saw me as a distraction from the work he was trying to do in that village. Even though I had experienced Jesus working in such powerful ways, and heard story after story of answered prayers, miracles and breakthroughs, I still found myself doubting that God was powerful enough to work through me and glorify his name despite the cultural barriers.

As my team walked along, holding children's hands and singing in unison, God's power and beauty were so evident. Yet my own fear of inadequacy kept me from trusting God and enjoying his glory. I prayed silently, asking God to help me reflect him more clearly. I asked him to use me, despite all the ways I didn't measure up. God answered that prayer in the sweetest way through Juancito.

We eventually approached a group of teenage boys on the side of the road. I had repeatedly tried to connect with these boys, but they had shown no interest. Instead, they were keen on taunting me (and other young women) with slurs and name-calling. Typically, the younger boys around them, Juancito included, would follow their lead. Playing games, singing or talking with us wasn't "cool" to the younger boys in those moments, because they wanted to impress the older boys. When I saw the teenagers sitting there, my heart sank. Jauncito was so peaceful in my arms, and I didn't want him to suddenly flip a switch and fight against my embrace. As we walked past the older boys, I braced myself. They sneered under their breath, as usual, then called out, *"Gringa!"* (that is, "Foreigner!"), followed by a bunch of laughter. Juancito jumped up and put his face right in front of mine. I expected him to mock me or scream at me along with the others, but what he actually did was drastically different. Juancito looked me in the eyes, and I saw that his were soft, tender and sincere. Then he took both of his hands and cupped them on my cheeks. He said, *"No eres gringa. Eres hermana."* Or in English, "You aren't an outsider. You are a sister." My heart broke in the best way, flooded with joy and humility. I hugged Juancito tight, and he settled back relaxed in my arms. I knew the moment was special at the time, but I didn't know just how meaningful that experience would be in my life going forward.

Juancito demonstrated the power of reaching out to another to offer support and understanding. Instead of drawing distinctions or viewing me as an outsider, he accepted me and focused on the common ground we shared. He has influenced how I view and communicate with people with different backgrounds and beliefs. Instead of focusing on our differences or my assumptions about others' beliefs and backgrounds, I practice concentrating on our shared humanity, and the joys and struggles that come along with that. When I approach a conversation with someone who shares different beliefs than my own, I try to keep these reminders at the forefront of my mind:

- Everyone needs to know that they are valued and that their life makes a difference.

- Everyone is on their own journey. Each of our paths are unique and valuable.

- Everyone tries to do their best with what they've been given.

- People believe what they do for a reason. There is a story behind how they think and what they believe.

- God is capable of intervening in others' stories in ways I can't perceive.

What reminders do you think would help you to find common ground and understanding with people of different backgrounds or beliefs?

ENGAGING IN DIALOGUE WITH GRACE

Most of the time, when I see stories on the news about a clash between Christian values and a cultural movement, there are plenty of indicators that neither side is looking for ways to understand the other. Rather, I see pointing fingers, stereotyping and shouting. These instances are usually blown out of proportion once they've taken the media stage, but how often do we partake in similar behaviors at the individual level? What stereotypes do you carry about people who are different from yourself? How do these assumptions affect your ability to have open and honest conversations? Are you part of the 87% of Christians who believe that it would be hard to have a normal conversation with Muslims or members of the LGBT community? Or the 85% of Christians who feel that way about atheists?[1] If so, it might be time to deconstruct the assumptions you have about these different groups, and rebuild your framework based on common ground and understanding, as we discussed in the last chapter. When the opportunity for conversation arises, we want to be prepared to pave the way for open conversations.

I have found Dee Allsop's list of approaches for finding common ground, which he shared at a conference called Q Commons, to be a great reference. Dee is a communications and positioning strategist with over 20 years of experience in the field, so he knows what he's talking about when it comes to finding common ground. He also contributes to "Q Ideas," a platform for exploring ways that Christians can engage the culture in redemptive ways. During a Q conference presentation, Dee provided a list of specific approaches for Christians to find common ground with people who think our faith is irrelevant or extreme.[2]

1. Begin the conversation with values/principles that most can agree on.

2. Look for areas of commonality and point out agreement.

3. Use metaphors cautiously, or avoid using them at all.

4. Ask questions of the other person, and be willing to accept the answer.

5. Summarize the other person's point of view to show you're listening.

6. Denounce extremists without silencing them, protecting their freedom of speech.

7. Give personal, relevant examples.

Another way to prepare for open conversations about faith and religion is to understand the larger picture of religion in America. To help us with this, let's turn to the U.S. Religious Landscape Study, designed and conducted by the Pew Research Center. Instead of simply ticking a box for a certain religion, the U.S. Religious Landscape Study conducted 35,071 phone interviews to get a more comprehensive understanding of people's affiliation and commitment to religion. The study was conducted in 2007 and again in 2014, which provided the ability to compare the data and identify trends and changes among religious identification in the U.S. The information that was gathered focused on the demographic characteristics of U.S. religious groups, their beliefs and practices, and trends such as religious switching (converting from one religion to another) and growing religious intermarriage rates.[3]

One of the Pew Research Center reports from this study looked specifically at the change in religious affiliation between the 2007 and 2014.[4] It found that the biggest change in religious affiliation was a drop in the percentage of Americans who identified themselves as Christian—almost an 8% drop from 2007 to 2014.[5] While the majority of the American population still identified as Christian, that 8% drop was significant. What happened to the 8% of the population who no longer identified as Christian?

The data showed that most of the people who dropped Christian affiliation did so in favor of no religion at all. As striking as the 8% drop in Christian affiliation is, there was an equally striking increase in the population who identified as "religiously unaffiliated". The religiously unaffiliated group includes those who describe themselves as atheist, agnostic or "nothing in particular;" they are sometimes referred to as "religious nones."[6] In the same period from 2007 to 2014, the population of those identifying as religiously unaffiliated rose 6.7%.[7] So it's the significant *decrease* of Christian affiliation along with the significant *increase* of "religious nones" that exposes a trend towards a post-Christian culture. The reality is, people are leaving the Christian faith to adopt a life with no religion at all.

The greatest factor that seems to influence the growth of "religious nones" is generation. While there has been growth in the religiously unaffiliated populations across all generations, Millennials have a drastically higher count than previous generations. Among younger Millennials (those born between 1990-1996), 36% describe themselves as religiously unaffiliated.[8] That's more than a third of younger Millennials! The older Millennial group (those born between 1981-1989) follows closely at 34%, which is also more than a third of the group.[9] These percentages are significantly high compared to Generation X or the Baby Boomers, whose "religious none" population was counted as 23% and 17% respectively.[10]

These statistics display the scope of Millennials who are currently unaffiliated with or uninterested in Christianity. While those numbers cast a gloomy picture of a trend away from Christianity, they aren't the full picture. One thing to remember about the Millennial generation is that they have a deep desire to live a life of meaning and purpose. This is true in both their personal life and career; Millennials look for opportunities that fuel a sense of purpose and importance.[11] Many Millennials want to experience something beyond themselves, bigger than themselves. They want to experience a transcendence deeper and longer-lasting than what they've found through sex, drinking, yoga or clean eating. Our vibrant, personal relationship with the living Jesus is the answer they've been looking for—they just might not know it if they haven't heard that kind of gospel before.

Drew Dyck, an author and editor for Moody Publishers, explains it this way:

> Millennials have a dim view of church. They are highly skeptical of religion. Yet they are still thirsty for transcendence. But when we portray God as a cosmic buddy, we lose them (they have enough friends). When we tell them that God will give them a better marriage and family, it's white noise (they're delaying marriage and kids or forgoing them altogether). When we tell them they're special, we're merely echoing what educators, coaches, and parents have told them their whole lives. But when we present a ravishing vision of a loving and holy God, it just might get their attention and capture their hearts as well.[12]

Most Millennials are in a season of life that is full of transitions, change and unknowns, whether they're in college, early career or early family life. These factors add to the list of questions they are already asking about purpose and meaning, which creates countless opportunities to relate to them, share stories and engage in dialogue. For example, as a friend struggles through the unknowns of a seemingly endless job hunt and aches for security, you can share your security in Christ. When a friend is in a bad relationship, but she's afraid to leave because she doesn't want to be alone, you can share the love and constant presence of God. When a friend struggles in his marriage and wants to give up, you can offer the hope and life-changing power of Christ.

There are literally endless possibilities for communicating the realness of Christ. And when you use your personal story, Christ's relevance will resonate in a new way. But in order for it to resonate, it needs to be shared. I know that that can feel scary or awkward. I understand the hesitations and questions that stop us from speaking up and sharing our hope. In those moments, when intimidation or insecurity strikes, remember that you have the Holy Spirit within you. You are not alone, and God gives you everything you need to walk in obedience with him.

WE'VE BEEN GIVEN EVERYTHING WE NEED

"But the fruit of Spirit is love, joy, peace, patience, kindness, goodness, faith, gentleness, self-control. Against such things there is no law." - Galatians 5:22-23

One of the things I find so amazing about our relationship with God is that, through Christ, he literally dwells within us as the Holy Spirit. The Bible is full of so many mind-blowing statements regarding the benefits of Christ living within us:

- We have the mind of Christ. (1 Corinthians 2:16)

- The same power that raised Christ from the dead now lives in us. (Romans 8:11)

- We are free from sin. (Galatians 5:1)

- We are alive with Christ. (Ephesians 2:5)

- We are coheirs with Christ. (Romans 8:17)

- Our bodies are temples of the Holy Spirit. (1 Corinthians 6:19-20)

- We have everything we need for godliness. (2 Peter 1:3)

That last one on the list always gets me. We have everything we need for godliness. *Really?* It doesn't always seem so. If I have everything I need for godliness, why am I still tempted to act in sinful, ungodly ways? Galatians 5 explains the dueling desires of the flesh and the Spirit within our hearts. The desires of the flesh, when acted on, lead to sexual immorality, moral impurity, promiscuity, idolatry, jealousy, outbursts of anger and selfish ambitions. On the other hand, the desires of the Spirit express themselves as love, joy, peace, patience, kindness, goodness, faith, gentleness and self-control. We usually call these expressions the "fruit of the Spirit."

For most of my life, I thought of the fruit of the Spirit as ideals. I considered them traits to strive for, but they always seemed to be out of reach. Then, a couple of years ago, a friend offered me a totally new, life-changing view on the fruit of the Spirit. We sat on the couch in her living room as she told me about a delicate situation in her life that had caused her great distress. She asked if we could pray about it, so we did so, right there on the couch. I prayed first, asking God to comfort her and give her discernment in handling the situation. When I finished, she began praying in a way I had never heard someone pray before. She claimed peace for her life. Every time I pray for peace in my own life, I think of the words of this friend. She prayed, "God, I know you've already given me peace. I have peace because I have Christ in me, and Christ is peace. Help me to recognize the peace you've given me. Help me to live in accordance to your peace. Show me the areas where I am not surrendering to your peace."

I learned through this prayer that peace isn't just an ideal or nice idea; it is a reality, and one to which we have full access. Feelings of stress, anxiety and discomfort are real, but the presence of these feelings does not mean that God's peace is absent. My prayer life and, quite frankly, my understanding of God have changed through my friend's prayer. I recognize now that the fruits of the Spirit are capable of operating at full-force in my life, but I need to willingly submit to them. This is true for all the fruits of the Spirit, not just peace. The expressions of Christ are always available to us; we just need to choose them over the expressions of our flesh.

The popularly-quoted phrase, "God will never give you more than you can handle," has always baffled me. What does it mean to "handle" something? The only definitive way I could think of to *not* "handle" something was death. But I don't think it aligns with God's heart to consider fighting exhaustion, hysteria, depression, addiction, apathy or hatred as "handling" it. Rather, I think that God intends for us to handle the trials we face by relying on the fruit of the Spirit we've been given. It means he doesn't put anything in our way that will stop us from finding our rest in him. We can have love, joy, peace, patience, kindness, goodness, faith, gentleness and self-control, no matter the circumstance. That is the gift of grace.

Notice, though, that the gift doesn't come without a call. We need to choose the fruit of the Spirit over the fruit of the flesh. To do so takes a great deal of humility and trust. The fruits of the Spirit are important to keep in mind when we think about sharing our stories and creating dialogue with non-Christians. Often, discussions regarding religion, beliefs or worldviews can grow heated quickly. It is easy to become offended and defensive if someone undermines your beliefs; if you don't consciously choose to respond from the Spirit, you will respond from the flesh. Certainly, there are times to boldly defend the name of Christ. However, if we choose to approach these conversations with humility and submission to the Spirit, we may find that our need to defend will be reduced while our message will be more clearly communicated.

Reflection Questions

1. What experiences have you had that expanded your understanding of people with different beliefs than your own? What did you learn from those experiences?

2. Why do you think so many Millennials have opted out of the Christian faith? Do you identify with any of their reasons for making that decision?

3. What situations do you most frequently see your friends struggling with? How might Christ be the answer to their pain? How do you think your story could be used to help a friend recognize the realness of God?

4. What fruits of the Spirit do you need to claim in your life today?

CHAPTER FOURTEEN

Starting the Conversation

*"Now there are different gifts, but the same Spirit. There
are different ministries, but the same Lord. And there are
different activities, but the same God activates each gift
in each person. A demonstration of the Spirit is given
to each person to produce what is beneficial: to one is
given a message of wisdom through the Spirit, to another,
a message of knowledge by the same Spirit, to another,
faith by the same Spirit, to another, gifts of healing by
the one Spirit, to another, the performing of miracles,
to another, prophecy, to another, distinguishing between
spirits, to another, different kinds of languages, to another,
interpretation of languages. But one and the same Spirit is
active in all these, distributing to each person as He wills."*
- 1 Corinthians 12:4-11

Just as the body of Christ equips us with unique skills and talents to glorify God, it also offers a plethora of ways to use our personal skill-sets and experiences to share the gospel with others. Your story is your story. It is special and powerful, and has so much potential to speak hope into despair and light into darkness. Do not discredit the way God has chosen to work in your life because of fear, insecurity or comparison. Rather, look for opportunities that are ripe for the message he has given you. Where can your story make the biggest impact? What struggles has he redeemed in you that you recognize in others? In this chapter, we will look at the beautiful examples of three of my friends—Cynthia, Rachel and Raquel—who share their stories and the life-changing truth of Jesus in powerful ways.

SHARING THE GOSPEL IS RECLAIMING WORTH

Cynthia is a woman on fire for Jesus. She is passionate about bringing his good news and love to the broken, especially women who have been victims of sexual exploitation. This is a calling she lives out through one-on-one mentorship relationships with victims and through her God-inspired non-profit, Free Ever After.[1] Free Ever After is a bridal boutique in Tucson. The boutique accepts donated, gently-used bridal gowns, and resells them to raise money to fight sex-trafficking and support victims coming out of the industry. Their heart is to reclaim wedding dresses—a symbol of love, purity and beauty—to redeem the value and dignity of women who have had those rights taken from them. The imagery is powerful, isn't it?

I first met Cynthia on a hot, July evening. We ordered our dinner at a Tucson restaurant, and chose to sit outside on the vacant patio to avoid the noise and distraction inside. We didn't waste any time getting to the heart of the conversation. Before our food even arrived, Cynthia was sharing her story with me. The strength, openness and the freedom she radiated captivated me. Cynthia shared the journey that led her to become so passionate about sexually-exploited women, and how she became inspired to start Free Ever After. When our food finally arrived, we didn't even touch it for forty-five minutes. I peppered Cynthia with questions and comments, and she continued sharing her beautiful story with me. I kept praying, "God, help me to remember all of this!" Cynthia's wisdom is deep. It is a joy to learn from her and see how she diligently lives out the passions that the Lord has placed on her heart.

Cynthia mentors women who have come out of prison on a probation program. Some of these women have been in prison for a long time, and they have lost everything and everyone—children, family and friends. They may not have anyone to support them as they work to re-acclimate and build a better life for themselves. The women in this program live in a house together, and they are provided with a variety of services to help them succeed in rebuilding their lives. While determining which services will be necessary, the women are interviewed to better understand their situations. If they have had any experiences with sexual exploitation (sexual assault, rape, prostitution, pornography, etc.), then Cynthia's mentorship becomes a requirement in their recovery process. Cynthia says the mentorship process itself is pretty simple: she and the woman meet together once a week to discuss a book about healing heart-wounds. But the simplicity of the program doesn't mean that the conversations, or breakthroughs are simple at all.

"Most of the women in the recovery program don't realize that they were victims. They have everything so mixed up regarding their worth. Many of them have come to believe that they made these destructive decisions themselves, or that they deserved what they got," Cynthia says. She tells me that her role is to listen to God and to speak life into the women. She asks God to help her to see the women with his eyes and to have his heart for them.

"We are Jesus to people when we just love them," she says. "When one of these women walks into the room, it's like the best, most beautiful thing in the world walked into the room." Take a moment to let that sink in. That's how Jesus sees us, and that's how Jesus sees the people around us. We are beautiful, precious and valued—no matter our back-story.

Cynthia explained to me that one of the barriers that she has to overcome when she first starts meeting with the women is their doubt of her ability to understand their stories at all. She says they call her a "square," and assume that her life is perfect with everything under control. To build trust with them and find common ground, Cynthia shares her own story of sexual exploitation and how it impacted her life. She makes her own brokenness clear, which opens the way for a more genuine conversation. But Cynthia also makes her hope and source of healing—Jesus—clear to the women she mentors.

For people who have been victimized, it can be extremely hard to see a different perspective. They may have believed lies about their worth and been stuck in the shame cycle for years and years. This is often the case for the women with whom Cynthia works. She says that helping them to reflect on their experiences to find a storyline is one of the most important parts of helping them get out of their shame cycle. Sexual exploitation is especially damaging to a person's self-value, and can severely warp how one thinks about herself, her exploitation and her own decisions. Cynthia shared stories of women who had been raped or taken advantage of as children, and then later went on to become prostitutes or join the pornography industry. For many of them, they bought into the lie that their worth was only in their body; they no longer recognized that they had been victims. Helping these women to understand and accept that their choice had been taken away from them is a first step in reclaiming their worth, Cynthia says. "When you work with them and coach them back to where the patterns originated, they can see that there was a cause."

I appreciate Cynthia's sensitivity towards these women, and it's something from which we can all learn. She truly wants to see these women's hearts healed and made whole again. Cynthia knows that this is possible in Jesus, but it's up to him to do the work. She says, "It's not about changing their behavior or righting the wrong choices they've made. It's about reclaiming their worth and dignity." Cynthia hears a lot of skepticism about God and Christianity from these women. Many are upfront with her right away, telling her that they aren't interested in what she has to offer. Cynthia doesn't let those remarks bother her or keep her from radiating Jesus within her. She says, "I just need to show them Jesus. I need to love them. And the way that makes them feel will open their hearts to listening to what I have to say." When the women aren't interested in Jesus, Cynthia tells them, "It's okay if you don't want Jesus. You don't have to." But if they want to know how Cynthia has been healed and transformed from her own hurtful past, "They know my answer is Jesus," she says.

Like Cynthia, we can use our own brokenness to relate to others in theirs. We don't need to have it all together or have all of the answers, but we can share the story of how Jesus has transformed us. He has lifted up our faces. He calls us by new names. We are beautiful and worthy to Jesus. That message is powerful. It meets a deep, deep need in the hearts of people who doubt their own worth.

SHARING THE GOSPEL CAN BE PLAYFUL

Evangelism is a central part of my friend Rachel's life and work. She leads a college ministry on a secular campus in Michigan.[2] This means that she spends a lot of time with students all across the faith spectrum: those who are skeptical and untrusting of religion, those who are passionate about following Jesus, and everyone in between (including people who hold religious beliefs other than Christianity). Now that I'm a few years out of college myself, I find myself fascinated by college ministry. College is such a unique season in life. The transitions and worldviews being shared are fertile grounds for questions of purpose, meaning and significance to arise. These questions can be the bedrock for spiritual conversations based on common ground and understanding.

If you grew up in the church, you may be familiar with the statistic that 60% of church-going youth leave the church after high school graduation. This may be true, and the reasons why are worthy of a discussion all their own. But the fact that young people are leaving the church in their college years does not negate the truth that people are also coming to faith in Christ for the very first time during their college years. *This* should really perk our attention.

What is it that draws competent, intelligent young people to adopt a faith in Jesus, right as the world tells them they have finally arrived at a life-stage when they can do whatever they want? It must be a relevant, life-changing relationship with a living God. Rachel shared about what it's like ministering to college students, and some of the ways she communicates a relationship with Jesus to people who don't know him. Her insights are key to identifying ways we can talk about God and share our faith with non-believers in our own lives.

One of the themes Rachel repeatedly brought up in our conversation was "playfulness." Now, I don't know about you, but playfulness isn't the first word I associate with evangelism. Far from it, actually. I think this is true for many Christians. We see evangelism as a duty, maybe even a weighty one. It's intimidating, and the stakes feel high. From Rachel's perspective, these associations stem from a misunderstanding of God, his delight in us and the joyful call he has given to us to share the gospel with others.

"Evangelism always starts with prayer," Rachel says. "But from there, it can take form in a lot of different ways. Spiritual conversations can spring up anytime, and we are more aware of the opportunities if we're looking for them," she adds. This anticipation and being on the lookout for opportunities to talk about spiritual matters is part of what Rachel means by "playfulness" in evangelism. "It's like an adventure," she says. A key element to engaging in evangelism as a playful adventure is security in our identity as God's children. When we know that God loves us and is there to help us, we are free to share him with more joy and confidence.

Another way that Rachel practices sharing a joyful gospel message is by expanding the view of the good news of Jesus. "My job isn't to make anyone 'feel convicted' about their sin on my terms, but to show how Jesus' grace and love is the solution to the problems they see and feel every day." When you know how God has worked specifically in your life, and you feel confident sharing your story, you can explain how God meets your needs daily. What are your daily difficulties? Loneliness? Anger? Abandonment? Anxiety? You can speak about these with the authority of your own life and the transformation you've experienced in Christ.

"People are asking big questions, whether out loud or just internally," Rachel says. "If we practice listening and being willing to take the next step, paying attention to what they are really saying, then we might be surprised by where the conversation leads." This is an opportunity to be playful, she says, "In situations like these, I'm often praying in my head, saying, 'Okay Jesus. I think I see this going somewhere. Give me the words to say, and help me to obey you. Help them to see your love.'"

As I talked with Rachel, I was encouraged by her enthusiasm and life-giving perspective on evangelism. But I also knew that she mentored several Christ-following students on campus, helping them find ways to share Jesus with their friends. I guessed that not all of them were so comfortable with the idea of talking about Jesus on a secular campus. I asked Rachel how she addressed the fears and concerns her students had, and what ways she coached them to overcome those hesitations.

Rachel confirmed that evangelism is always a journey with her students. Sometimes, students are eager to share their hope with others, but more often, they have questions and doubts about how to start a spiritual conversation and share Jesus in a relevant way. "Learning evangelism isn't always a big, revolutionary change," she says. "A lot of times, it looks more like a series of small 'yeses.'" Saying "yes" to sitting by someone who looks like they may be lonely, saying "yes" to asking a follow-up question and responding thoughtfully, saying "yes" to going out of your way to show love to another person and let them know that they matter. These small "yeses" build up, and may even create opportunities to say "yes" to asking what someone believes in, sharing your own hope in Jesus or even offering to pray for the other person.

When students look for examples of how to relate to others

and find common ground with them, Rachel sends them to the example of Jesus. "He never shared truth with someone in the same way twice," she says. While there are evangelism formulas out there that may "work," lasting change starts when people find a solution for a real problem they already experience, Rachel says. This is why using your story to open up a conversation about the real issues and hardships you face can be so powerful. If trust is created and the other person is comfortable sharing their pain or struggles with you, you have an opportunity to offer the very real hope of Jesus.

You have the potential to spark that hope in someone else's heart. It's not up to you whether they choose to follow Jesus. Always remember that. It is the Holy Spirit who transforms the heart—we are only called to be faithful in sharing God's love and sharing the gospel of hope. Jesus is real and moving, and we get to play a part in sharing that good news. That is something worth celebrating with a heart full of joy, not duty.

SHARING THE GOSPEL IS SHARING YOUR HOPE

The summer after I moved to Tucson, I met my friend Raquel. We got to know each other quickly when we both helped lead a camp for our church's high school youth group. Camp friends bond quickly, no matter your age, and Raquel's friendship has continued to be influential and encouraging in my life ever since. I have been especially challenged by Raquel's dedication to seek out opportunities to share Jesus with the people in her life. In every conversation we have, Raquel tells me about something new she's learned or a situation where she shared the gospel with someone. Her example is so beautiful to witness, and such an encouragement to me.

Unlike the above examples of Cynthia and Rachel, Raquel doesn't work in a ministry-based position. She is a hair-stylist at a local salon, but she views her whole life as a ministry. No matter what your daily life looks like—whether you're an engineer, stay-at-home mom, teacher or a student—people around you are looking for the hope, love and security you have in Christ. I spoke with Raquel about some of the ways she interweaves her relationship with God into her day-to-day and makes him a natural part of her conversations.

One of the things that Raquel makes an effort to do is to point the glory back to God when she is applauded for something she's done well. "Generally, I'll say something like, 'Thanks. But all the glory goes to God,' 'Thanks, but it wasn't me. That was all God,' or, if it was something I said, I'll say, 'Those weren't my words, they were God's.'" Raquel told me that for her, it's easy to include God into her conversations because she is so aware of how intricately he is working in her life. "I've learned how involved God is in the details of life, and knowing that, I just can't take the credit for myself. So my first thought is to give God praise and thanks for working through me," she says.

I was curious what types of responses Raquel had experienced from sharing her faith in these ways. "When I'm saying something like this around family or other believers, they agree in acknowledgement. That's really special, because it cues me to stop and enjoy God's presence for a moment." Isn't that beautiful? Personally, I sometimes miss those opportunities. When I am with other believers, I may be lazy about actually acknowledging God, because I assume that we're all on the same page. But in fact, acknowledging God's involvement is an additional opportunity to praise him and multiply the glory he receives.

On the other hand, when Raquel directs the glory to God in conversations with non-believers, she isn't without hesitations. "I always feel excited about the opportunity to glorify God. But I also feel worry and fear: 'What are they going to think?' 'What are they going to say?' 'Are they going to think I'm weird for saying that?'" She says she knows those thoughts aren't from God, so she prays for the courage to speak them despite her fears. "I've never actually had someone question me or jump into a spiritual conversation right after saying something like that, but that's okay," she says. "It's God's job to open up the opportunities, and we can trust that he will use our words to raise curiosity about himself," she adds.

Raquel's awareness of God and his involvement in her life go beyond directing the glory off herself and onto Christ. It also affects her sensitivity to the difference Christ has made in her own life. This helps her to relate to people in a meaningful and authentic way. Raquel says, "I know the difference Christ makes because I've lived without him. I know what I looked like, what I sounded like, and who I was before Christ." Recognizing that difference plays a big part in how Raquel shares her own story and invites others to share theirs with her. Raquel told me the following story about sharing Jesus with a woman with whom she works:

I noticed a girl at work who was feeling a little down. When I had a moment, I followed her into the breakroom and saw that she was crying. I asked her what was wrong, which led into a conversation. She was having problems with her boyfriend and didn't know what to do. She was really dependent on him, and found her worth in him. I was able to share Jesus and his hope with her. It was one of the coolest moments! We prayed together, and it was actually her first time praying. Following her into that breakroom was not my idea. That's not something I would have done on my own. But by stepping out in faith, I was able to have this conversation with her.

My co-worker opened up pretty easily when I asked her questions. I asked her, "Where do you find your hope?" I have found that, generally, people's responses to this question are something in this world. This girl shared that in her case, it was her boyfriend. So I was brutally honest with her. I know it could have very much turned her off, but I shared the reality that things in this world will always disappoint us. I know what it's like to look to the things of this world for hope, but it just doesn't work out. It would have been easy to think, "Oh, she won't want to open up to me. I don't know her well enough." But we'd be surprised by how much people want to connect, especially when they don't have the hope of Christ and the security of that relationship. My co-worker was willing to share with me, which was so awesome!

I asked Raquel to share a few tips to become more aware of the open doors God may present us with in the day-to-day. Here are her encouragements to you:

1. **Pray.** Always pray first. Pray for courage. Pray for opportunities to talk about God and acknowledge him. Pray for the people with whom you will come in contact. Even when you don't know who those people will be, God does.

2. **Read the Bible.** Read it and pray for understanding as you do so. The more you understand the Word, the more you will be able to live it out.

3. **Understand just how much Jesus has changed your life.** There are real consequences for people who don't know Jesus, so being okay with not sharing the Gospel to others is dangerous.

4. **Consider people's eternal destinations.** No matter where someone is on his or her journey now, their destination could very well be heaven. But they need to be introduced to Jesus to arrive there.

There are so many ways to share the gospel, and so many opportunities to share your story. I hope that Cynthia, Rachel and Raquel's stories inspire you to look for the open doors to which God may lead you. The knowledge of God's redeeming love is not ours to hold onto, kept secretly hidden in our hearts. It is a gift meant to be shared.

Reflection Questions

1. Do you relate to any of the stories or methods of sharing the gospel that Cynthia, Rachel or Raquel shared? If so, what resonates? If not, why not?

2. What situations have you confronted that provided an opportunity to speak value and dignity to someone else? What was their reaction? How did you feel?

3. What decisions do you face today with the option to say "yes"? How do you think God could use your small "yeses" for something much bigger than you imagine?

4. Think back on your past week. What opportunities did you have to direct glory back to God? What is a natural way you could attribute glory to God in future conversations?

Reflection Questions

CHAPTER FIFTEEN

The Send-Off

You have so many ways to share your story. No matter what life stage you are in, what your day-to-day looks like or what your means are, you have a sphere of influence on which you can leave your mark. Whether or not you are intentional about it, your life creates a legacy. You have the choice to determine if that legacy will point back to you, or if you will point it back to God. This could be in big ways or small, but the point is, your story makes an impact. Starting now, in whatever life circumstances God has given you, you have the opportunity to share your hope with others. When you share your story and explain the relationship you have with Christ in a relatable, authentic way, God is glorified.

I have shared some examples of people who own and share their stories well, but I encourage you to look around yourself. Who in your life can you learn from? Which people encourage you to live more fully for Christ? What examples of story-sharing have deeply moved you?

When you chose to share your story, doing so won't always feel easy. Even if you have a strong desire to share the gospel with non-believers, the confidence you have in your story will likely ebb and flow, depending on the season. It's important to be prepared for those more difficult times. Our emotions can easily deceive us. We can mistake fear for a reason to not follow through on a conviction, or confuse embarrassment for condemnation. We need to take account of our feelings and insecurities, choosing actions based on truth and trust, not fear. The great part about taking courageous steps is that every time you choose to be brave, bravery becomes more natural. You can actually inspire yourself to pursue a courageous lifestyle by sharing your story. And while you're at it, you'll be inspiring those around you as well.

Living courageously requires us to take our stories seriously. It requires us to believe that we have purpose and a calling, and that isn't always easy. Because honestly? It's a lot easier when we don't take ourselves seriously. It's easier to sell ourselves short and play small. It's easier to play the victim than to live as an overcomer. It's easier to disqualify ourselves than genuinely try to find common ground and share your story.

For a long time, I believed that living in this small way was best. I thought it represented the qualities I admired, like humility, grace, patience and gentleness. But recently, my views have changed. The Lord has opened my eyes to a higher calling—one in which I can walk in humility, grace, patience and gentleness, while also displaying strength, discernment, wisdom and leadership. What I used to see as a dichotomy, a choice between gentleness and strength, I now see as fruit of the same seed. That seed is Christ living in me. He is both my strength and my song. He calls me on the journey and equips me with what I need. He calls me to live my life for his cause, and sometimes, that requires being brave and speaking up when I would rather stay quiet. Sometimes, it means that I am uncomfortable and need to enter uncharted waters.

I'm getting used to that feeling as I make a habit of being brave. I'm getting used to taking my life seriously, remembering that Christ was serious when he died on the cross for my sins and called me to follow him. Taking that call seriously is a daily challenge, but it's also chock-full of blessings, joy and purpose. And I hope that you're willing to take seriously your story and your role in the conversation, too. Learning to understand and share your story is a great place to start. As you finish this book, I want to leave you with a few final encouragements and a roadmap to get you started on sharing your story.

THE NEXT STEPS

GIVE YOURSELF TIME

My hope is that reading this book has been a reflective process for you. I hope that as I shared pieces of my story, you were able to relate and think of similar ways you have grown in your walk with Christ. However, understanding your story and all its intricacies is a process. It's not a one-and-done deal. Rather, it is a lifelong process of reflection and growth. I hope that this book encourages you to adopt such a lifestyle. Discovering and owning your story is about learning to integrate the truths you know about God with your real-life experiences.

We are constantly growing, changing and learning new things. Our stories and our reasons for believing what we do grow and change, as well. To continue integrating your understanding of God with your experiences, it's good practice to regularly reflect on the following questions: How do you see yourself growing? What do you feel God is speaking to you? How do you handle difficult situations? What do you admire in others? What confuses you about God?

As you reflect on these questions, you will grow more comfortable speaking about their answers with others. You will be more prepared to share your story when the opportunity presents itself.

PRACTICE FINDING COMMON GROUND

Finding common ground is the aspect of sharing your story that will likely require the most practice. Depending on your upbringing, you may have been taught to notice differences in others before accounting for your similarities. In many Christian circles, there is strong emphasis on "the world" and its corruption. Approaching every conversation with this mindset won't get us very far in creating meaningful connections with others.

Look around your social circles. If you realize that you're surrounded only by other Christians, it might be time to look for opportunities in your community to get involved in and meet people with different faiths and backgrounds. You'll never understand the other side of the conversation unless you actually get to know the people behind the conversation. Maybe there is a volunteer opportunity for a cause you are passionate about? It doesn't need to be a formal arrangement or a big time commitment. Maybe you could get to know the fellow patrons or baristas at the coffee shop you frequent? Or maybe you could join a community sports team? When Trevor and I moved to Tucson, we joined a community kickball league that played every Thursday night. It gave us the opportunity to make friends with people of different backgrounds than our own, which was valuable in many regards.

Aside from actually meeting and talking with people different from me, one of the ways I practice finding common ground is by paying attention to the news. Most evenings after work, Trevor and I will have long discussions about news stories or current events. We ask questions we don't know the answers to, and then practice reconciling our faith and experiences with the issues at hand.

This practice has taught me so much. It has helped me to articulate my faith and integrate it with my worldview. I am much more confident sharing what I think and believe because I know that they are my own thoughts and beliefs, not ones that have been fed to me. I have found it especially helpful practicing this with Trevor because we help each other see the faults or oversights in our line of thinking. It's never easy to be challenged, but it is so good for us. If articulating your beliefs feels intimidating or impossible, maybe you could benefit from something similar. You can even practice this on your own while listening to or reading the news. When you hear a statement or opinion on the news that you don't agree with, try putting yourself in the place of someone who would agree with the statement. Then ask yourself the following questions: What circumstances would make someone think this way? How can you relate to them? How would you explain your beliefs without sounding ignorant or condescending? When this practice becomes second nature, you will be able to find common ground with almost anyone.

START SHARING

Sooner or later, you'll recognize an opportunity to share your story, and I hope that you take it. Even if your throat dries up, your palms sweat and your voice comes out shaky at first, I hope you choose to be courageous with your story. Don't confuse the physical and emotional responses of vulnerability with weakness. Choosing vulnerability is not only strong—it's powerful. It's powerful because vulnerable and authentic moments connect us. When you open up to share your experience, or explain your beliefs in a wholehearted manner, you take away the need for others to put up walls. How you approach sharing your story will affect the way people listen to your story.

You will never be able to control how someone responds when you share your story or explain your faith, but you can create an atmosphere in which they feel safe to discuss, rather than defend. Trust that God has entrusted you with your life experiences for a reason. Celebrate the ways he has changed you. Stay humble and cognizant that your story is ultimately about God, for his glory. When you keep those three things in mind, your story will communicate hope. You never know just how badly someone else may need that hope.

INVITE OTHERS TO SHARE THEIR STORIES

A rewarding part of sharing my story has been how it has opened up the door for people to share their stories with me. I sometimes feel like my heart is a treasure trove of beautiful stories that friends have shared with me. Trust is built quickly when you share your story. It is the foundation on which hard questions are asked and counsel is sought. We cannot anticipate the blessings that may result. Trust invites people to share their own story. And when they do, you will be ready to listen, empathize and encourage them in their journey because you have already learned how to do so with your own.

CLOSING PRAYER

"Not to us, Lord, not to us but to your name be the glory, because of your love and faithfulness." - Psalm 115:1

Thank You!

Thank you to my parents, David and Susan Voss, for loving and supporting me in all of my endeavors. I have learned so much about commitment, perseverance and making the most out of life from your example. Your abundant generosity and willingness to serve others is something I hope my own life reflects. Thank you to my sister, Kellie Voss, for being the best role model a little sister could ask for. You live life to the fullest, and it is so fun to see. Thank you for sacrificially pouring hours into this book, helping me clean up the grammar and spelling mistakes. I love how great of a team we are, and how you gently challenge me to continually improve. Erica Male, thank you for inspiring me to put my dreams into action. Watching you do so yourself, with such grace and boldness, moves me. Your love and enthusiastic encouragement have been a drumbeat to keep me going throughout this project. Denis Male, I admire your kind heart and thoughtfulness with your words. I'm so glad to have you as a brother.

To Todd and Connie Spoelma, thank you for raising the most kind-hearted, considerate and supportive man I have ever met. I am so thankful that by marrying Trevor, I also got to join your beautiful family. Thank you for regularly checking in on the status of the book and motivating me to see it through. To Tyson, Troy and Tori Spoelma, I love you all. I'm proud and grateful to be your sister.

Thank you, Ashleigh Dewitt, for speaking life into this book from its inception. You believed in me before I believed in myself, and your encouragement and guidance carried me through to completion. Thank you for reading my early, horribly rough drafts and giving me practical advice for improving my writing and clarifying the message. Your fingerprints are all over this book. I'm blessed to have you as a cousin-friend.

Thank you, Meaghan O'Connor, for seeing beauty in the early drafts I shared with you. The way you reached out and offered your help to me was such a testament to God's goodness, providence and faithfulness. You are wise, passionate and so gifted. Thank you for sharing your talents with me, and helping me determine which topics to dive into, and which to leave by the wayside.

Thank you, Taylor Lange, Alyssa Scheidel, Allie Marie Smith and Gabriel Gonzalez, for sharing your stories and perspectives with me. I am so grateful you allowed me to share them in this book. Thank you, Judy Nauta, Cynthia Magallanes, Rachel Gregg and Raquel Gonzalez, for letting me interview you and learn from you. Your stories shaped the writing of this book in many ways. Thank you for letting me share your insights with others. Each of you has left such a mark on my heart and life, and I know the Lord better because of you.

Thank You!

Thank you to my grandparents, Kathleen Robinson and the late Bill Robinson, Joe and Beverly Koutny and Ron and Peggy Voss, for your love and prayers. Thank you for building the beautiful families I am so proud to be part of. To my Great-Grandma Schroeder, thank you for your legacy of prayer and loving the Lord. Tell It Well is being published on your 102nd birthday—Happy Birthday!

To my friends and family all over the world: I wish I could give each of you a shout-out by name, but there are just too many of you! Thank you for sharing your lives with me and accepting me as I am. Thank you for your support and cheering me on as I've written Tell It Well.

Thank you to my wonderful Book Launch Team. It was humbling and oh-so-encouraging to have you behind me from the very moment I told the world that I was starting this project. Thank you for answering my surveys and questionnaires, and for sharing your own experiences with talking about your faith. Your feedback was extremely helpful to me as I wrote this book.

To all my friends in Tucson's Tuesdays Together group: Thank you for teaching me how to create something beautiful. I continue to learn so much from each of you and I am astounded by the community we have created. Thank you for everything.

To all the members of the Tovar RC: Wow. Thank you for praying big on my behalf when I was tired and overwhelmed. We witnessed a miracle! It is such a gift to be surrounded by friends like you, who challenge Trevor and I in our walks with the Lord. What a blessing it is to experience community with you.

Thank you, Kevin Welch, for modeling servant-leadership to me. I'm so grateful for your intentionality in teaching me to lead others well. Tell It Well would never have existed if it weren't for your guidance and support as I created "Your Story Weekend" during our time together at Higher Ground. Maddie Baker, thank you helping me be a better follower of Christ. Our time in ministry together, and your friendship, has influenced my life so much. I admire your strength, passion for the Lord and leadership.

Thank you, David Kinnamon and Gabe Lyons, for your needed and insightful books, UnChristian and Good Faith. They were extremely helpful resources to me as I wrote Tell It Well. Thank you also for the work you do separately, David at Barna Group and Gabe with Q Ideas. You are meeting significant needs through those platforms, and I am grateful to learn from you myself.

Finally, thank you to my husband, Trevor. I am the luckiest woman in the world to walk through life with you. The significance of your role in this book is impossible to describe. You have seen all the messy, the tears and moments when I nearly gave up. But your steadiness, silliness and dedication to excellence always worked together to keep me grounded. You are God's greatest blessing in my life, and it is a deep joy to share this adventure with you. I love you with all my heart, forever and always.

To the Lord my God: This book is from you, through you and for you. Thank you for calling me to this endeavor and leading me ever-so-gently through all the uncertainties. Your grace is amazing. Use this book however you'd like to bring glory to your name. I love you.

Thank You!

THANK YOU TO EVERYONE WHO MADE TELL IT WELL POSSIBLE:

Aaron C Clark & Allyssa M Clark
Abby Hunefeld
Alexa Iwaniuk
Alexandria Jester
Alexis Datema
Alisia
Alyssa
Alyssa Gallion
Alyssa Scheidel
Amanda Akgul
Amanda Hall
Amanda Reese
Amanda Sweedyk
Amber Barnett
Amy Paegel
Andrea Koskinen
Andrew & Lindsay Sisson
Anna Guthrie
Ashleigh Dewitt
Ashley Esper
Barb Chase
Becca Robinson
Bev
Brad & Alexis Zeinstra
Breanna L. Sherrow
Brooke McDonald
Caleb
Caleb & Andi Richardson
Callie Opper
Carrie
Cassandra Opper
Catherine Zietse
Cecilia Wallace
Chris Hsieh
Christa Formberg
Christine
Dad & Mom
Daphna
David & Renae
Debbie Cooke
Denis Male & Erica Male
Derek & Heather Sterenberg
Du & Alexandria Bui
Dustin Tramel
Elizabeth Victory
Emily DeHaan

Emily Dillon
Emily Lindman
Emma LaMore
Emma Richardson
Fabiola Bedoya
Florence A. Karine
Gretchen Driesenga
Hannah Van Dyke
Jace Watland
Jaclyn Reinink
Jacob & Samantha Bylsma
James & Carol Spoelma
Jane from PatronPress
Jehricole Olenzuk
Jessica Kooienga
Jillayn Malburg
Jimmy and Kate
Joe & Bev Koutny
John & Shirley
Judy
Julia Hilbrands
Julie Barrett
Julie Ellens
Kait Masters
Kari
Karina
Kate Mills
Katelin H
Kathleen Robinson
Katie
Katie Delaney
Kayla Gorst
Kellie K. Voss
Kelsey Klumpstra
Kimberly Schulz
Kristiana Daniels
Kury
Larry & Tammy Fredeen
Laurie DeLong
Lexy Ward
Liza Fongers
Lois Richardson
Lori Faith
Maria Roate
Martha Warriner Jarrett
Mary Flynn
Mary Simon

Meaghan O'Connor
Megan
Meghan Jordon
Michelle Robinson
Morgan Kelley
Moriah Hazeltine
Natasha Rulason
Nicolet Groen
Niki Wagner
Nikki Fisher
Nitya
Olivia Horrell
Olivia Ruckstuhl
Penny Marchand
Rachel Gregg
Rachel Wozniak
Randy Richardson
Raquel Gonzalez
Rebecca De La Paz
Rebecca Hout
Rebekah Postema
Ron & Teresa Wind
Sam Brace
Sara
Serena Ellens
Shari
Shirley Westveer
Stacy
Stephanie Nauta
Stephanie Robinson
Steve & Lindsey Burkey
Steve & Sue Bradt
Susie
Suzanne Reinink
Taylor Elizabeth Lange
Teresa
The Wozniaks
Theresa Delaney
Todd, Connie, Troy & Tori Spoelma
Tom & Sue Robinson
Toryanna DeYoung
Trevor Spoelma
Trudy Bloem
Valerie Lurye
Wendy
Zach & Charlotte Yentzer

Notes

CHAPTER 1: WHAT IS YOUR STORY?

1. Psalm 115:1 (NIV).

CHAPTER 2: WHY YOUR STORY IS IMPORTANT

1. See (Good Faith, 42).
2. See (Good Faith, 43).
3. See (Good Faith, 43).
4. See (Apologetics).
5. John 6:44a.
6. 2 Corinthians 4:6.
7. See (America's Changing Religious Landscape).
8. Ibid.
9. See (Good Faith, 45).
10. See (Good Faith, 44).
11. Deuteronomy 31:6.

CHAPTER 3: COMMON MISCONCEPTIONS ABOUT SHARING YOUR STORY

1. Philippians 4:6-7.
2. Romans 6:1-2.
3. Isaiah 41:10.
4. John 3:16.
5. See (Lewis, 40).
6. See (Stanton).

CHAPTER 4: FINDING A STORY IN THE FOG

1. See (Jesus Culture).
2. See (Smith).

CHAPTER 5: EMBRACING MY STORY

1. www.jenuinelife.com
2. 2 Corinthians 10:5.
3. See (Augustine, 95).
4. See (Bonhoeffer, 44).

CHAPTER 6: THE POWER OF LOOKING FORWARD

1. Philippians 1:6.
2. 2 Corinthians 1:22.
3. John 8:31-36.
4. See (Hurnard).
5. Romans 5:3-5 (NIV).
6. 1 Corinthians 13:13 (NIV).

7. Romans 5:3-5 (KJV).
8. John 16:33.
9. 2 Corinthians 5:7.
10. See (Hurnard, 93).
11. John 16:33.
12. Hebrews 6:19.
13. Romans 5:1-5 (NIV).
14. Romans 5:5.
15. Hebrews 11:1.

CHAPTER 7: MAKING SENSE OF YOUR STORY

1. See (Delistraty).
2. See (Pennebaker and Seagal).
3. Ibid.
4. Ibid.
5. See (Brown, 50).
6. Psalm 139:1-6.
7. Proverbs 16:9.
8. Psalm 57:2.

CHAPTER 8: OWN YOUR STORY AND GIVE GOD THE GLORY

1. Matthew 6:11.
2. Ephesians 3:18-19.
3. Matthew 14:16.
4. 1 Timothy 2:4.
5. Isaiah 61:1.

CHAPTER 9: ROOT YOUR IDENTITY

1. Timothy 3:16.
2. Psalm 19:7.
3. See (Tozer, 1).
4. Ephesians 1:11-12.
5. Psalm 34:18.
6. Psalm 68:20.

CHAPTER 10: BOUNDARIES DON'T MAKE YOU COLD

1. See (Brown, 122).
2. See (Brown, 123).
3. See (Brown, 123).
4. 2 Corinthians 9:5.
5. 2 Corinthians 9:6-9.
6. 2 Corinthians 9:10-12.

7.   2 Corinthians 9:13-15.
8.   See (Authentic).
9.   See (Chapin).
10. Ibid.
11. Psalm 34:18.

CHAPTER 11: FINDING COMMON GROUND

1.   See (Bryant).
2.   John 13:35.
3.   Exodus 4:10.
4.   Genesis 18:9-15.
5.   Genesis 43:30.
6.   Book of Song of Solomon.
7.   Daniel 1:8-20.
8.   Jonah 4.
9.   Book of Psalms.
10. Joshua 1:9.
11. Exodus 4:1.
12. Exodus 4:11-12.
13. Exodus 4:14.

CHAPTER 12: LISTEN FIRST, THEN ENGAGE IN DIALOGUE

1.   See (Ferris).
2.   Ibid.
3.   See (Our Faith, World Vision).
4.   See (About Us, World Vision).
5.   See (Our Work, World Vision).
6.   See (Our Faith, World Vision).
7.   See (Good Faith, 42).
8.   See (Unchristian, 156).
9.   See (Good Faith, 212).
10. Daniel 1:17-21.

CHAPTER 13: ENGAGING IN DIALOGUE WITH GRACE

1.   Barna OmniPoll.
2.   See (Allsop).
3.   See (America's Changing Religious Landscape).
4.   Ibid.
5.   Ibid.
6.   Ibid.
7.   Ibid.
8.   Ibid.

9. Ibid.
10. Ibid.
11. See (Adkins).
12. See (Dyck).

CHAPTER 14: HOW TO START THE CONVERSATION

1. Learn more at: www.freeeverafter.org.
2. Learn more at: www.givetoiv.org/rachel_gregg

Works Cited

"About Us." World Vision, www.worldvision.org/about-us. Accessed 20 Sept. 2016.

Adkins, Amy. "What Millennials Want From Work and Life." Gallup. 11 May 2016, www.gallup.com/businessjournal/191435millennials-work-life.aspx Accessed 01 Oct. 2016.

Allsop, Dee. "Finding Common Ground." Q Commons, Q Ideas 2015. Lecture.

"America's Changing Religious Landscape." Pew Research Center, 12 May, 2015, www.pewforum.org/2015/05/12/americaschanging-religious-landscape/. Accessed 25 Sept. 2015.

"Apologetics." Merriam-Webster. www.merriam-webster.comdictionary/apologetics. Accessed 9 Oct. 2016.

Augustine, Saint. Confessions. Translated by Henry Chadwick, Oxford University Press, 1991.

"Authentic." Merriam-Webster. www.merriam-webster.com/dictionary/authentic. Accessed 11 Oct. 2016.

Barna OmniPoll, August 2015, N = 1,000.

Bonhoeffer, Dietrich. The Cost of Discipleship. Touchstone, 1995.

Brown, Brené. Rising Strong. Spiegel & Grau, 2015.

Bryant, Eric. "Encounter: Overcoming Us vs. Them." ChurchLeaders. www.churchleaders.com/outreachmissions/outreach-missions-blogs/149540encounter_overcoming_us_vs_them.html. Accessed 01 Oct. 2016.

Chapin, Angelina. "Sober Is the New Drunk: Why Millennials Are Ditching Bar Crawls for Juice Crawls." The Guardian. 21 Apr. 2016, www.theguardian com/society/2016/apr/21/millennials-booze-free-events-juicecrawl-newyork. Accessed 20 Sept. 2016.

Delistraty, Cody C. "The Psychological Comforts of Storytelling." The Atlantic. 2 Nov. 2014. www.theatlantic.com/health/archive/2014/11/the-psychological-comforts-of-storytelling/381964/. Accessed 20 Sept. 2016.

Dyck, Drew. "Millennials Need a Bigger God, Not a Hipper Pastor." Aspen Group. 3 July 2014, www.aspengroup.com/blog/millennials-need-a-bigger-god-not-a-hipper-pastor. Accessed 01 Oct. 2016.

Ferris, Elizabeth. "Faith-based and Secular Humanitarian Organizations." International Review of the Red Cross, vol. 87, no. 858, 2005. www.icrc. org/eng/assets/files/other/irrc_858_ferris.pdf.

Hurnard, Hannah. Hinds' Feet on High Places. Living Books ed., Tyndale House Publishers, 1986.

Holy Bible. Holman Christian Standard Version. Holman Bible Publishers, 2009.

Jesus Culture. "Your Love Never Fails." Your Love Never Fails, Jesus Culture Music, 2008.

Kinnaman, David, and Gabe Lyons. Good Faith: Being a Christian When Society Thinks You're Irrelevant and Extreme. Baker Books, 2016.

Kinnaman, David, and Gabe Lyons. Unchristian: What a New Generation Really Thinks about Christianity ...And Why It Matters. Baker Books, 2007.

Lewis, C. S. Mere Christianity. HarperCollins ed., HarperSanFrancisco, 2001.

"Our Faith." World Vision, www.worldvision.org/our-work/faith-in-action. Accessed 20 Sept. 2016.

"Our Work." World Vision, http://www.worldvision.org/our-work. Accessed 20 Sept. 2016.

Pennebaker, James W., and Janel Seagal D. "Forming a Story: The Health Benefits of Narrative." Journal of Clinical Psychology, vol. 55 no. 10, 1999, pp. 1243-254.

Smith, Allie Marie. Wonderfully Made: Becoming Who You Are in Christ. Group, 2012.

Stanton, Glenn. "FactChecker: Misquoting Francis of Assisi." The Gospel Coalition, 10 July 2012, www.thegospelcoalition.org/article/factchecker-misquoting-francis-of-assisi.

The Holy Bible. New International Version. Zondervan House, 1984.

Tozer, A.W. The Knowledge of The Holy. HarperOne, 1961.

CPSIA information can be obtained
at www.ICGtesting.com
Printed in the USA
BVHW03s0216080218
507615BV00001B/65/P